Sustaining *and* Defending *the* Faith

Joseph Fielding McConkie
Robert L. Millet

Sustaining
and Defending
the
Faith

Bookcraft
Salt Lake City, Utah

Library of Congress Catalog Card Number: 85-72074
ISBN 0-88494-572-3

First Printing, 1985

Printed in the United States of America

Contents

Preface

As the night follows the day, so opposition follows truth. The promised "restoration of all things" has witnessed the revival of all past arguments against God's earthly kingdom along with the spirit of antagonism known to the Saints of all dispensations past. "It seems," said Joseph Smith, "as though the adversary was aware, at a very early period of my life, that I was destined to prove a disturber and an annoyer of his kingdom; else why should the powers of darkness combine against me?" (JS—H 1:20).

The Church was but weeks old when Joseph Smith was arrested on charges of being a disorderly person and setting the country in an uproar by preaching the Book of Mormon. The arresting constable was to have delivered him into a mob ambush, but, impressed with his character, instead aided his escape. Two farmers—men of integrity, James Davidson and John Reid—were retained to defend the Prophet, which they did successfully. "But alas!" as Reid told the story, "the devil, not satisfied with his defeat, stirred up a man not unlike himself" to go to the adjoining county and obtain a writ against Joseph there. Allowed neither food nor rest, Joseph was immediately taken captive by the arresting officer. "He took me to a tavern," Joseph recounted, "and gathered in a number of men, who used every means to abuse, ridicule and insult me. They spit upon me, pointed their fingers at me, saying, 'Prophesy, prophesy!' and thus did they imitate those who crucified the Savior of mankind, not knowing what they did."[1]

Friends of the Prophet again sought Davidson and Reid to defend him. "I made every reasonable excuse I could," John Reid said, "as I was nearly worn out through fatigue and want of sleep; as I had been engaged in law suits for two days, and nearly the whole of two nights. . . . While Mr. Knight was pleading with me to go, a peculiar impression or thought struck my mind, that I must go and defend him, for he was the Lord's *anointed*. I did not know what it meant, but thought I must go and clear the Lord's *anointed*. I said I would go, and started with as much faith as the Apostles had when they removed mountains, accompanied by Father Knight, who was like the old patriarchs that followed the ark of God to the city of David.''[2]

Of the second trial Joseph Smith said: ''Many witnesses were again called forward and examined, some of whom swore to the most palpable falsehoods, and like the false witnesses which had appeared against me the day previous, they contradicted themselves so plainly that the court would not admit their testimony. Others were called, who showed by their zeal that they were willing enough to prove something against me, but all they could do was to tell something which somebody else had told them.''[3] These trials were but the pattern, the prototype, of that which the future would witness a thousand times over, though the enemies of the Church would quickly learn that printer's ink was safer than public cross-examination.

Of his attorneys the Prophet said: ''They spoke like men inspired of God, whilst those who were arrayed against me trembled under the sound of their voices, and quailed before them like criminals before a bar of justice.''[4] This too prefigured many a future scene.

That quiet yet unmistakable voice which whispered to John Reid and directed him to go and defend the Lord's anointed has whispered and will yet whisper in like manner to many others. As he went in faith, so must they. And as he and James Davidson spoke with a power beyond their own, so have and will countless others in the defense of the faith and the Lord's anointed. It is to those who would be true to the faith that this book is written. In so doing it has not been our purpose to respond to specific questions or challenges—these are endless. We have little interest in theological dogfights. Settling a dispute among the Nephites, Christ said, "He that hath the spirit of contention is not of me, but is of the devil, who is the father of contention, and he stirreth up the hearts of men to contend with anger, one with another" (3 Nephi 11:29). We have no interest in pursuing such a spirit. Rather, it is our desire to teach correct principles, principles which properly understood not only respond to specifics but show the inconsistency and sham of our antagonists' questions. A proper understanding of gospel principles is the most eloquent and effective defense of the faith.

The saving principles of the gospel of Jesus Christ are not in flux; they do not change from day to day or from age to age. Those truths that brought salvation to the ancients will bring salvation to those of our day. The manner in which those truths were opposed anciently foretells the manner in which they have been and are opposed in our day. What argument is there that has been brought against the Book of Mormon that cannot be brought against the Bible with the same results? What argument is there that can be brought against Joseph Smith that cannot be brought against Jesus Christ or the ancient prophets and Apostles with the same results? What stone is there than can be hurled at The Church of Jesus Christ of Latter-day Saints that, if thrown back, does not destroy more in its return?

Can we claim loyalty to the Bible and reject the Book of Mormon, saying that surely God would never command one man to take the life of another? How could we ever be expected to accept the story of Nephi and Laban? Might we ask, What of Elijah, the great Bible prophet who killed four hundred and fifty of the priests of Baal in one afternoon and twice called down fire from heaven that consumed fifty soldiers sent to escort him to the king (see 1 Kings 18 and 2 Kings 1)? Is it consistent and is it honest to reject the Doctrine and Covenants with the argument that changes were made in the revelations when it is common knowledge that the New Testament is a compilation of five thousand different manuscripts, no two of which are the same? Doesn't that suggest that someone changed something? Yet we still accept it as scripture. Is there not some irony to be found in that spirit which mocks Joseph Smith in the same language that was used to mock and taunt Jesus the Christ?

Many of Christ's disciples left him after his bread of life sermon, leading him to ask of the twelve, "Will ye also go away?" It was Peter, as their spokesman, who responded, "Lord, to whom shall we go? thou hast the words of eternal life. And we believe and are sure that thou art that Christ, the Son of the living God." (See John 6:66–69.) We feel to respond in the same manner to the many who would torch the kingdom with the fire of their wrath today and would turn us out of the true fold—"To whom shall we go?" What do they offer us in exchange for priesthood, keys, and sealing power, for a God who speaks, prophets who live, and the promise of everlasting life?

CHAPTER 1

Strength in Opposition

On the sixth of April 1845 the Twelve Apostles issued a proclamation which included these words: "As this work progresses in its onward course, and becomes more and more an object of political and religious interest and excitement, no king, ruler, or subject, no community or individual, will stand *neutral*. All will at length be influenced by one spirit or the other; and will take sides either for or against the kingdom of God."[1]

There is no neutrality where Christ and his kingdom are concerned. Light and darkness will never meet; Christ and Satan will never shake hands. The kingdom of God will always be opposed by the kingdom of the adversary. The Saints of God in all dispensations have had the sure promise that they and the gospel of which they testify will be known for good and evil. It is the validity of their testimony that draws the fire. Error can be a part of the ecumenical movement abiding in peace, truth cannot. Truth is identified both by the witness of the Spirit and the opposition of the adversary.

A Sign by Which Truth Is Known

When Moroni first appeared to Joseph Smith he called
Joseph by name, and then introduced himself as a messenger
from the presence of God. He then told the youthful prophet
that the Lord had a work for him to do and that his name
would be had ''for good and evil among all nations, kindreds,
and tongues, or that it should be both good and evil spoken
of among all people'' (JS—H 1:33). Such were the words with
which he introduced both Joseph Smith and the Church that
he would yet restore to their destinies. No more remarkable
prophecy can be imagined. Consider its implications: the
promise was that people of all nations, kindreds, and tongues
on the face of the earth would hear his name—some would
speak of it with honor and with respect, while others would
speak of it with derision and scorn. Now let us ask what are
the chances that such a prophecy will come to fruition? What
are the odds? What is the statistical probability? Suppose, for
instance, we randomly choose some seventeen-year-old boy
from the local community and then prophesy of him that his
name will yet be known among every kindred, tongue, and
people. What are the chances of that actually happening?
How many people are there in earth's history of whom that is
true? And yet even that would not fulfill the prophecy, for the
person so chosen must be known for ''good and evil.'' Some
must honor and revere him while others speak of him in
terms of aspersion and insult.

If further perspective is needed, one might be asked to
name the founders of the half-dozen most prominent religious
denominations in America today and recite something good
and evil about each of them.

Let it be remembered that this was a frontier boy without
fortune, social standing, or the benefit of anything more than
the rudiments of an education. How similar was a prophecy
made by a girl of the same approximate age some nineteen
centuries earlier. She, too, was without fortune or social

standing; she, too, was unknown to her fellow countrymen and lived in a tiny obscure village; and she, too, confidently proclaimed that all future generations would call her blessed (see Luke 1:48). Such was the prophecy of a young girl from Nazareth of Galilee, who was destined to give birth to the Christ child.

Of his experience in the sacred grove Joseph Smith wrote,

> I soon found . . . that my telling the story had excited a great deal of prejudice against me among professors of religion, and was the cause of great persecution, which continued to increase; and though I was an obscure boy, only between fourteen and fifteen years of age, and my circumstances in life such as to make a boy of no consequence in the world, yet men of high standing would take notice sufficient to excite the public mind against me, and create a bitter persecution; and this was common among all the sects—all united to persecute me.
>
> It caused me serious reflection then, and often has since, how very strange it was that an obscure boy, of a little over fourteen years of age, and one, too, who was doomed to the necessity of obtaining a scanty maintenance by his daily labor, should be thought a character of sufficient importance to attract the attention of the great ones of the most popular sects of the day, and in a manner to create in them a spirit of the most bitter persecution and reviling. But strange or not, so it was, and it was often the cause of great sorrow to myself. (JS—H 1:22–23.)

And so it was that as Moroni concluded his instructions to Joseph Smith that September night in 1823, he said he would give the young prophet a sign by which he might know that all that had been promised and prophesied would come to pass. The sign was that when it became known that the Lord had shown these things to him, the workers of iniquity would seek his overthrow. Moroni explained they would "circulate falsehood to destroy your reputation, and also will seek to take your life." Yet Joseph was assured that his life would be preserved so that he might accomplish his mission despite the persecution that he was assured would rage increasingly against him and his work. Moroni further said that the iniquities of men would be revealed and that "those who are not built upon the Rock will seek to overthrow this church; but *it will increase the more opposed.*"[2]

True to Moroni's prophecy, when the priesthood was restored, the Church was organized, missionaries were sent forth, and the ordinances of salvation were reintroduced to the children of men, the slumbering hosts of hell were awakened and the winds of hatred began to blow. One bitter storm of religious wrath followed another, in the midst of which we find the Lord speaking to the Prophet Joseph, who had for months been illegally incarcerated in a dungeon ironically called Liberty Jail. "The ends of the earth shall inquire after thy name," came the voice of heaven, "and fools shall have thee in derision, and hell shall rage against thee." Then came the assurance that the sun indeed shone above the smog of sectarian hatred, for the Lord said: "The pure in heart, and the wise, and the noble, and the virtuous, shall seek counsel, and authority, and blessings constantly from under thy hand." (D&C 122:1–2.)

The Testimony of History

"Every man to whom the heavens have been opened and who has received revelations from God has been hated by his fellows; his life has been sought, and he has had no peace on the earth," testified George Q. Cannon. "No matter how numerous such persons have been they have been hunted and driven. So true is this that Stephen the martyr, when being stoned to death, taunted the Jews with their unbelief and the acts of their ancestors. Said he, 'which of the prophets have not your fathers persecuted? and they have slain them which showed before the coming of the Just One.' "[3]

The death of Joseph Smith did not bring an end to the bitterness that opposed him or the faithful Saints. Brigham

Young and those that followed him became the heirs of hell's wrath. Joseph F. Smith explained:

> It has ever been the desire of the wicked to destroy the people of God. They have never slackened their efforts, nor failed to use all the means in their power, nor hesitated to resort to the most cruel, foul and fiendish acts to accomplish their nefarious purpose. This same cruel enmity, although for the time being, to some extent subdued or held in check by the Almighty, still smoulders and rankles in their hearts, awaiting a favorable opportunity to burst forth as fiercely as at any time during the life of the Prophet Joseph. This is one of the strongest evidences we can have of the divine mission of President Brigham Young. Because of the inspiration of the Almighty and power of God which has rested upon him and accompanied his administrations, he has been the very centre of the target at which all the deadly weapons of the enemy has been aimed ever since the death of the Prophet Joseph. I say this is one of the strongest evidences we can have of this fact, aside from the testimony of the Holy Spirit, which bringeth knowledge. It is unmistakable. The hatred of the wicked always has and always will follow the Priesthood and the Saints. The devil will not lose sight of the power of God vested in man—the Holy Priesthood. He fears it, he hates it, and will never cease to stir up the hearts of the debased and corrupt in anger and malice towards those who hold this power, and to persecute the Saints, until he is bound.[4]

The student of Church history will remember that many groups have claimed to be the rightful successor of Joseph Smith. Among these are the Rigdonites, Strangites, Bennettites, Wightites, Gaddenites, Cutlerites, Morrisites, Josephites —in fact, we have had all manner of *ites.*

Now, in which of these has the world shown an interest? Which were hounded and maligned as Joseph and his followers have been? None! And why? Because they no longer had the priesthood or the truths of salvation. As Joseph F. Smith explained: "They have deserted the cause, have struck hands alike with the infidel and the bigot, and formed an alliance with the maligners and persecutors of the Saints, and therefore they are harmless in the eyes of the world and of their *master* whom they blindly list to serve.''[5]

President Spencer W. Kimball has testified: ''If this were not the Lord's work, the adversary would not pay any attention to us. If this Church were merely a church of men and women, teaching only the doctrines of men, we would encounter little or no criticism or resistance—but because this is the Church of Him whose name it bears, we must not be surprised when criticism or difficulties arise.''[6]

Approaching God

When Joseph Smith sent the first missionaries to the British Isles, the inspiration of that action was immediately attested by satanic opposition. Illustrating this, Heber C. Kimball recounted the events that surrounded the first baptisms performed in that land. This took place in Preston, England, on Saturday, July 29, 1837, after it had been agreed that Elder Kimball was to perform baptisms the next morning in the Ribble River, which runs through Preston.

> By this time the adversary of souls began to rage, and he felt determined to destroy us before we had fully established the kingdom of God in that land, and the next morning I witnessed a scene of satanic power and influence which I shall never forget.
>
> Sunday, July 30th (1837), about daybreak, Elder Isaac Russell (who had been appointed to preach on the obelisk in Preston Square, that day), who slept with Elder Richards in Wilfred Street, came up to the third story, where Elder Hyde and myself were sleeping, and called out, 'Brother Kimball, I want you should get up and pray for me that I may be delivered from the evil spirits that are tormenting me to such a degree that I feel I cannot live long, unless I obtain relief.'
>
> I had been sleeping on the back of the bed. I immediately arose, slipped off at the foot of the bed, and passed around to where he was. Elder Hyde threw his feet out, and sat up in the bed, and we laid hands on him, I being mouth, and prayed that the Lord would have mercy on him, and rebuked the devil.

While thus engaged, I was struck with great force by some invisible power, and fell senseless on the floor. The first thing I recollected was being supported by Elders Hyde and Richards, who were praying for me; Elder Richards having followed Russell up to my room. Elder Hyde and Richards then assisted me to get on the bed, but my agony was so great I could not endure it, and I arose, bowed my knees and prayed. I then arose and sat up on the bed, when a vision was opened to our minds, and we could distinctly see the evil spirits, who foamed and gnashed their teeth at us. We gazed upon them about an hour and a half (by Willard's watch). We were not looking towards the window, but towards the wall. Space appeared before us, and we saw the devils coming in legions, with their leaders, who came within a few feet of us. They came towards us like armies rushing to battle. They appeared to be men of full stature, possessing every form and feature of men in the flesh, who were angry and desperate; and I shall never forget the vindictive malignity depicted on their countenances as they looked me in the eye; and any attempt to paint the scene which then presented itself, or portray their malice and enmity, would be vain. I perspired exceedingly, my clothes becoming as wet as if I had been taken out of the river. I felt excessive pain, and was in the greatest distress for some time. I cannot even look back on the scene without feelings of horror; yet by it I learned the power of the adversary, his enmity against the servants of God, and got some understanding of the invisible world. We distinctly heard those spirits talk and express their wrath and hellish designs against us. However, the Lord delivered us from them, and blessed us exceeding that day.[7]

When Heber C. Kimball had the opportunity to relate this experience to Joseph Smith, he asked the Prophet what it meant, desiring to know if they had done anything wrong to cause the manifestation.

" 'No, Brother Heber,' he replied, 'at that time you were nigh unto the Lord; there was only a veil between you and Him, but you could not see Him. When I heard of it, it gave me great joy, for I then knew that the work of God had taken root in that land. It was this that caused the devil to make a struggle to kill you.'

"Joseph then related some of his own experience, in many contests he had had with the evil one, and said: '*The nearer a person approaches the Lord, a greater power will be manifested by the adversary to prevent the accomplishment of His purposes.*' "[8]

The Greater the Truth, the Greater the Opposition

Satan stands in opposition to truth: the greater the truth, the greater his opposition. The greatest heresies always stand opposite the greatest truths. Since the greatest truths in all eternity are the truths about God, it naturally follows that the greatest heresies are those that deny his existence or that direct worship to false gods. The three greatest truths in all eternity are those truths concerning God the Father, God the Son, and God the Holy Ghost. Immense effort has been made in the kingdom of darkness to hide, obscure, or pervert our knowledge of each of these divine beings.

The greatest of all truths is that God is our eternal Father, that he is a personal being, and that we have in reality been created in his image and likeness—that we are his spirit children, and that we have within us the innate capacity to become like him. The greatest heresy ever devised is that heresy which defines the nature and being of God as that of a spirit essence filling the immensity of space, being everywhere and yet nowhere; it is the heresy that God is without body, parts, and passions, that he is incomprehensible, uncreated, and unknowable. Out of this web of darkness every apostate Christian creed has been spun. It is a doctrine of hopelessness and despair, a doctrine made of the darkness of the kingdom from which it comes.

The second greatest truth of all eternity is that Jesus the Christ is in reality the Son of God, that he is our Lord and our Redeemer. Because of him we are ransomed from the effects of temporal or physical death, and we may be ransomed from the effects of spiritual death by obedience to the laws and ordinances of his gospel. Thus, the second greatest heresy known to man is the doctrine that denies his divine sonship, that ignores his example in advancing from grace to grace, that refuses to recognize that it is obedience that calls forth the blessings of heaven, and offers in its stead that "salvation" proposed in the heavenly councils by perdition himself, who asked of us nothing more than petitions of praise.

The third of the world's greatest heresies is that which denies the role of the Holy Spirit as a revelator. Because all true religion is revealed religion, and because God can be known only by revelation—and must be so known by each individual—it is an essential element of false religion to seal the heavens, when necessary admitting revelation to those of the past, but always denying it to those of the present.

The Discerning of Spirits

Since the organization of the Church in 1830, literally millions of people have left the various churches of Christendom to join The Church of Jesus Christ of Latter-day Saints. In so doing they have shared a common feeling of joy and excitement about what they have found in the restored gospel. By the tens and hundreds of thousands, they and their children have served as missionaries. They have gone first to family and then to friends to share what they have found. In the countless times that this drama has been enacted, we know of no instances in which these converts have been impelled to vilify and attack the churches they left. We know of no books written for that purpose, no movies made to that end, and in the thousands of meetings we have attended we have never heard a single sermon in which that was done. In contrast, many members of the Church have had experiences with those who have chosen to leave Mormonism but who cannot leave it alone. The preoccupation of their lives becomes barbs, attacks, misrepresentations, and the like. We simply suggest that we discern the spirit of their actions and words. What is the source of bitterness, ugliness, meanness? Is this of God or of some other source, and if of another, what?

As teachers at the Church university, the authors have had in their classes scores of young people who have joined the Church despite considerable opposition on the part of friends and family. Stories of parental bitterness, of being disinherited or disowned are not uncommon. And again we would ask the question, What is the source of such feelings? When young men or young women say to their parents, "We have decided to join The Church of Jesus Christ of Latter-day Saints," this means they will commit themselves to being morally clean, to keeping the Sabbath holy, to being honest and upright in their dealings with their fellowmen, to refraining from the use of drugs (except for medical purposes), alcohol, and tobacco. It means they will give of their own time to the service of others and that when they marry they will do so with a commitment that is not only for time but for eternity, and they will seek to raise a good family. It means they will not only seek to honor their parents, but to honor and obey the laws of the land. When children choose this and their parents become bitter and angry, again we would suggest we ought to "discern the spirits" and ask from whence comes the opposition.

A mission president overseas was invited by a group of the nation's leading ministers to speak to them on the subject "What right do Mormons have in our country?" He accepted their invitation and introduced his remarks by suggesting that, as he understood it, everything that was virtuous, lovely, or of good report came from one source, that being God, while those things that represented bitterness, ugliness, rancor, and so forth came from an opposite source, that being the devil. He asked them if that was according to their understanding. All agreed. He then said, "Now if any of you have any of those feelings of meanness in your heart toward me or my church, where did you get them?" His audience sat appropriately silent, for in the weeks previous each had done and said much about the missionaries and the Church that evidenced the spirit which they were serving.

Conclusion

One does not approach God without the adversary's opposition. The opposition of darkness and evil is a sure sign that the path being followed is offensive to the prince of darkness and thus pleasing to the God of heaven. We repeat the great lesson learned from the Prophet: "The nearer a person approaches the Lord, a greater power will be manifested by the adversary to prevent the accomplishment of His purposes." To this we add the admonition of Elisha to his servant, who feared because of the greatness of the army that surrounded Israel. "Fear not," he said, "for they that be with us are more than they that be with them." Then he implored the Lord to open his servant's eyes so that he might see the legions of heaven's army standing in readiness. (See 2 Kings 6:15–18.)

As Moroni said of the Church, "it will increase the more opposed," so it can appropriately be said of its members. Even in opposition there is that which strengthens and edifies. We have two witnesses of the divine mission of the Prophet Joseph Smith and the Church he restored: first, that born of the Holy Ghost quietly conveyed through the spirit of peace; and second, that born of the spirit of the adversary, loud in railing accusation.

CHAPTER 2

If Christ Came Today

There is no originality in hell. There are no new ways to oppose truth. The same spirit that opposed Christ in the meridian of time would oppose him were he to come today. The opposition would be the same, the spirit the same, and the arguments the same—and the Savior's fate would be the same. The opposition against Joseph Smith and the restored gospel is a mirror reflection of the opposition against Christ and the gospel in the meridian of time.

A Profile of God's Servant

You are invited to test your knowledge by identifying the servant of God described with the following clues:

1. His family was often in trouble and moved about a good deal.

2. His parents were described as being of the lowest social class and as having the loosest of morals.

3. As a young man he said things that astonished and disturbed people.

4. Local ministers stirred up trouble and spread scandalous reports about him and his family.

5. He claimed to be the agent of God chosen to restore the gospel in its purity.

6. He preached to those who professed to have the way of life leading to salvation, not to the heathen who professed no belief in God.

7. The greater part of the people of his day rejected him and his message while claiming a belief in the prophets of past ages.

8. He was rejected in the name of God and by the use of scriptural arguments.

9. The most bitter opposition against him was incited by the religious leaders of his day.

10. He was eventually killed by those who were angry and bitter with him for his teachings and what he professed to be.

These clues describe Joseph Smith and Jesus of Nazareth equally well. There is a remarkable similarity in the lives of both men. It is not without significance that while among the Nephites the resurrected Christ took passages from the writings of Isaiah, passages that described his mortal ministry and suffering, and applied them anew to the Prophet Joseph Smith. (See 3 Nephi 20:43–46; 21:9–10.)

We anticipate that if we had preserved for us the words that Christ's enemies said and wrote about him to compare with what our contemporary opponents of truth have written and said and are yet writing and saying about Joseph Smith that they would be remarkably similar. Indeed, we expect that such opponents would need only to replace the name *Jesus of Nazareth* with the name *Joseph Smith* and they would be ready to go to press.

Illustrating that our expectation is not far from the truth, Hugh Nibley summarized the literature about Christ as follows:

All sources, early and late, Christian and anti-Christian, agree that Jesus' family was often in trouble and moved about a good deal. The early anti-Christian writers made much of this: a family of improvident ne'er-do-wells, tramping about the country looking for odd jobs; Mary, a woman of the lowest classes and the loosest morals, working as a ladies' hairdresser, kicked out by her husband when she had an affair with a Roman soldier (they furnished the name, rank, and serial number), giving birth in disgrace to Jesus, the ambitious boy who picked up a bag of magic tricks in Egypt along with exalted ideas about His own divinity, and who gathered about Him a band of vagabonds and desperadoes with whom He ranged the countryside picking up a living by questionable means. [1]

The early Christian accounts of Jesus and his doings were, scholars tell us, written in reply to the scandalous stories that were spread concerning his youth and his family. Nor can it be much of a surprise to us as to who were writing and circulating these nefarious tales—"it was the doctors of the schools, the same Scribes and Pharisees who relentlessly pursued Jesus and John the Baptist during their ministries."[2] Nibley concludes his article by noting, "The Latter-day Saint reader cannot but note striking parallels between the early anti-Christian scandal stories and the Palmyra tales about the Joseph Smith family."[3]

Religious Leaders Rejected Christ

The picture painted by the Gospel writers is one in which we find Christ in constant conflict with those professing righteousness—it was the religious leaders who were most offended by him. When there was conflict we always find scribes, Sadducees, or Pharisees present. The scribes were the ordained scholars who clearly saw Jesus as a threat to their craft. Sadducees and Pharisees were the two major religious parties of the day, albeit comparatively few people were actively involved with them. In all the nation of Israel their combined numbers never approached ten thousand. It ought to also be noted that there was a bitter spirit of rivalry between them. The only matter upon which they were ever able to agree was to oppose Christ, his followers, and his doctrines (for example, see Matthew 16:1).

In the eyes of these religious zealots Christ could do no
right. "But whereunto shall I liken this generation?" he
asked. "It is like unto children sitting in the markets, and
calling unto their fellows, and saying, We have piped unto
you, and ye have not danced; we have mourned unto you,
and ye have not lamented. For John came neither eating nor
drinking, and they say, He hath a devil. The Son of man came
eating and drinking, and they say, Behold a man gluttonous,
and a winebibber, a friend of publicans and sinners. But
wisdom is justified of her children." (Matthew 11:16–19.)
Shall we paraphrase his words, that their full impact may find
expression in modern idiom—" 'What illustration can I
choose to show how petty, peevish, and insincere are you
unbelieving Jews? You are like fickle children playing games;
when you hold a mock wedding, your playmates refuse to
dance; when you change the game to a funeral procession,
your playmates refuse to mourn. In like manner you are only
playing at religion. As cross and capricious children you
reject John because he came with the strictness of the
Nazarites, and ye reject me because I display the warm
human demeanor that makes for pleasant social intercourse.' "⁴

Under the guise of loyalty to the law of Moses, these disciples of man-made tradition sought Christ to kill him. His
offense? He healed a man on the Sabbath day, thus rejecting
the rabbinic doctrine that to aid the body in healing itself was
to cause the body to work and thus violate the injunction that
no work be done on the Sabbath. Yet they could not refute
Christ's simple logic when he reminded them that they would
circumcise a child on the Sabbath so that the law of Moses
would not be violated. How then could it be an affront to
Moses or God to do a greater work of righteousness and make
a man whole on the Sabbath? (See John 7:19–23.) So in their
pretended offense at his having violated the law, they justified

themselves while totally disregarding that law's precept and purpose as they sought his death.

These same leaders, in violation of their own law, had Christ arrested and tried in their church courts. Disregarding all the rights of the accused they found him guilty of blasphemy and condemned him to death. Ironically his death came at the hands of the civil court, or the court of Rome in the form of Pontius Pilate, who asked these priests, these spiritual leaders of the nation, "Shall I crucify your King?" to which they responded: "We have no king but Caesar" (see John 19:15). Thus, in contriving the death of the Messiah they committed the very sin of blasphemy for which they had condemned him.

Tradition and Feigned Loyalty to Dead Prophets

Christ was rejected and killed in the name of piety and of loyalty to the law he himself had given Moses on Sinai. He was killed by those professing the right and authority to lead their nation in worship of him and to guide them into his presence. Thus the "doctors of the law" made "broad their phylacteries," and enlarged "the borders of their garments" (signs of their piety and righteousness), they built the "tombs of the prophets" and garnished "the sepulchres of the righteous," they reverenced dead prophets and rejected living ones, substituting traditions for commandments. Of them Christ said: "Ye made the commandment of God of none effect by your tradition. Ye hypocrites, well did Esaias prophesy of you, saying, This people draweth nigh unto me with their mouth, and honoureth me with their lips; but their heart is far from me. But in vain they do worship me, teaching for doctrines the commandments of men." (Matthew 15:6–9.)

Those who rejected Jesus as the Christ did so while professing a great love for the scriptures and a loyalty to prophets of ages past. Thus we find Christ challenging them to search the scriptures—"for," he said, "in them ye think ye have eternal life." They thought their ability to quote scripture, their feigned loyalty to dead prophets, and their observance of ritual would be enough to save them. But Christ declared it was not. He taught that devils may quote scripture, advocate loyalty to dead prophets, and love to substitute ritual for righteousness. Christ's message to his detractors was that if they would search the scriptures with a sincere heart and real intent, they would discover that the very scriptures they were using to reject him were testifying of him. (See John 5:39.) Further, he told them that not he, but Moses, would stand to condemn them on the day of judgment, for it was in the excuse of loyalty to Moses that they rejected the Savior of mankind. Moses' sole purpose had been to testify of him. Obviously they had not understood that message, for Christ accusingly questioned: "But if ye believed not his writings, how shall ye believe my words?" (John 5:47; see verses 40–47.)

Those of Christ's day professed that had they lived in the days of their fathers, they "would not have been partakers with them in the blood of the prophets." Christ testified that their actions in rejecting him evidenced just the opposite. "Wherefore ye be witnesses unto yourselves, that ye are the children of them which killed the prophets." And so he said in reference to his pending death at their hands, "Fill ye up then the measure of your fathers." (Matthew 23:30–32.)

Such is the pattern. Living prophets are invariably rejected in the name of loyalty to dead prophets. To those possessing the same spirit in his day, the great Lamanite prophet Samuel said:

> And now when ye talk, ye say: If our days had been in the days of our fathers of old, we would not have slain the prophets; we would not have stoned them, and cast them out.
> Behold ye are worse than they; for as the Lord liveth, if a prophet come among you and declareth unto you the word of the Lord, which testifieth of your sins and iniquities, ye are angry with him, and cast him out and seek all manner of ways

to destroy him; yea, you will say that he is a false prophet, and that he is a sinner, and of the devil, because he testifieth that your deeds are evil.

But behold, if a man shall come among you and shall say: Do this, and there is no iniquity; do that and ye shall not suffer; yea, he will say: Walk after the pride of your own hearts; yea, walk after the pride of your eyes, and do whatsoever your heart desireth—and if a man shall come among you and say this, ye will receive him, and say that he is a prophet.

Yea, ye will lift him up, and ye will give unto him of your substance; ye will give unto him of your gold, and of your silver, and ye will clothe him with costly apparel; and because he speaketh flattering words unto you, and he saith that all is well, then ye will not find fault with him. (Helaman 13:25–28.)

History Repeats Itself

It is not difficult for the student of the New Testament to anticipate how the message of the gospel restoration in our day will be received by modern persons possessed of a spirit akin to that of the ancient Sadducees and Pharisees. Espousing tradition as their source, they claim allegiance to a God who is without body, parts, and passions; a church without prophets, Apostles, or revelation; a heaven without place in time or space; and a resurrection without a body. Of the spirit behind such traditions and creeds the Prophet Joseph Smith said it has "filled the world with confusion" and is the "very mainspring of all corruption," causing the whole earth to groan under the weight of its iniquity. "It is an iron yoke," he said, "a strong band; they are the very handcuffs, and chains, and shackles, and fetters of hell." (D&C 123:7–8.) Of the professors of religion who have exchanged the promised blessings of heaven for money, or who offer those blessings without even the necessity of obedience and righteousness, would we not expect to hear the Lord say that "all their creeds were an abomination in his sight" and that their "professors were all corrupt"? Would it not be appropriate for him to say of them as he had of those of his day, " 'they draw near to me with their lips, but their hearts are far from me, they teach for doctrines the commandments of men, having a form of godliness, but they deny the power thereof' "? (JS—H 1:19.)

And would we not expect the honest in heart to be looking for the fulfillment of Jeremiah's prophecy that Israel will gather from among the nations of the earth saying: "Surely our fathers have inherited lies, vanity, and things wherein there is no profit. Shall a man make gods unto himself, and they are no gods?" And the Lord will speak, saying, "Therefore, behold, I will this once cause them to know, I will cause them to know mine hand and my might; and they shall know that my name is The Lord." (Jeremiah 16:19—21.)

And would we not expect them to respond to Joseph Smith as they have to prophets and faithful followers of Christ in all ages—as the book of Hebrews records—with "mockings and scourgings, yea, moreover of bonds and imprisonment: They were stoned, they were sawn asunder, were tempted, were slain with the sword: they wandered about in sheepskins and goatskins; being destitute, afflicted, tormented; (Of whom the world was not worthy:) they wandered in deserts, and in mountains, and in dens and caves of the earth." (Hebrews 11:36—38.)

We are reminded that Jesus challenged those who sought to kill him, saying: "Many good works have I shewed you from my Father; for which of those works do ye stone me?" In response the Jews said: "For a good work we stone thee not; but for blasphemy; and because that thou, being a man, makest thyself God." Jesus answered by quoting a portion of Psalm 82:6, which states, "Ye are gods; and all of you are children of the most High." He then asked, in essence, "If you claim to believe in the scriptures and they say that we are all the children of God, how can I be accused of blasphemy for saying that I am the Son of God?" (See John 10:32—36.) That the scriptures sustained him was a matter of no concern to these feigned lovers of the word of God, for their social standing and precious traditions were being challenged.

Thus we feel impressed to ask concerning the Prophet Joseph: For what good work was his life so often sought? What was it that incited his enemies' murderous hatred? Was it the claim that he had seen the Father and the Son? Was it the fact that he healed the sick and cast out devils? Was it his professing that he had entertained angels? Or was it the bringing forth of the Book of Mormon as a second witness of Christ? Why, we ask, was his testimony and work so threatening? Wherein is the concern if one does not believe his testimony? When Peter and John were brought before the council of the Jews, Gamaliel, an honorable man, reasoned that they ought be left alone: "For," said he, "if this counsel or this work be of men, it will come to nought: But if it be of God, ye cannot overthrow it." (Acts 5:38–39.)

The honest in heart in Jesus' day asked, If Jesus is not the Messiah, when the Messiah comes what will he do that Jesus has not done? (See John 7:31.) And again we are led to ask, if Joseph Smith is not the great prophet of the restoration, when that prophet comes what can he do that Joseph Smith did not do? And what of the prophecies of Isaiah and Ezekiel and the Psalmists that a book was to "spring forth" from the earth to help in gathering Israel and testifying of Christ? If the Book of Mormon is not that book, then we anxiously await another to come forth in the manner of the Book of Mormon and teaching the doctrines taught in the Book of Mormon.

The murder of Joseph and Hyrum Smith at Carthage, Illinois, "was not a spontaneous, impulsive act by a few personal enemies of the Mormon leaders, but a deliberate political assassination, committed or condoned by some of the leading citizens in Hancock County." Their murder was the work of a "respectable set of men" who sought to justify their deed with the argument that they had acted in accordance with "the higher law of community approval" and thus in the best interest of all.[5] Be it remembered that Christ told his Apostles that the time would come that "whosoever killeth you will think that he doeth God service" (John 16:2).

The trial of the acquitted murderers of Joseph Smith has been appropriately summarized as follows: "For the anti-Mormon defendants tried and acquitted at Carthage, the jury, as voice of the community, had provided a ceremonial cleansing by which the defendants could return to society absolved of the stigma of murder and fully qualified to function in a community soon to be rid of the Mormons. Many years later, when Thomas C. Sharp was asked after a long and creditable career in politics and government in Warsaw if he had murdered Joseph Smith, his only response was fully relevant— 'Well, the jury said not.' The democratic version of the higher law—popular sovereignty—had been applied to his case; its spokesman, the jury, had fully exonerated him of any sense of guilt."[6]

So consistently have living prophets been rejected in the name of loyalty to dead prophets that it is difficult to imagine hell without a church on every corner, each espousing its loyalty to some particular doctrine or theological champion while rejecting the fulness of the gospel and the testimony of living prophets. In the great revelation on the degrees of glory Joseph Smith described those in the telestial kingdom: "For these are they who are of Paul, and of Apollos, and of Cephas. These are they who say they are some of one and some of another—some of Christ and some of John, and some of Moses, and some of Elias, and some of Esaias, and some of Isaiah, and some of Enoch; but received not the gospel, neither the testimony of Jesus, neither the prophets, neither the everlasting covenant." (D&C 76:99–101.) That is, they had their doctrine, they had their prophet, and they claimed loyalty to the scriptures, yet they rejected the Lord's servants—but did so carefully in the name of reverence to the past and love of the gospel.

We Receive Christ by Receiving His Servants

Having charged the Twelve Apostles with their ministry to teach and testify of him, Christ told them that "he that receiveth you receiveth me, and he that receiveth me receiveth him that sent me" (Matthew 10:40). To receive the Apostles meant to accept them as the mouthpiece of Deity, recognizing their voice as his voice and their authority as his authority. One cannot accept the Father while rejecting the Son, and one cannot accept the Son while rejecting those he has commissioned to act in his name. To reject Peter, James, and John, or any of the Twelve, was at the same time a rejection of Christ. One cannot, in honesty, profess to accept Christ while rejecting those whom he has sent to teach and testify of him, and to whom he has given the priesthood or authority to act in his name and perform the ordinances of salvation.

"Whether by mine own voice or by the voice of my servants, it is the same," the Lord said (D&C 1:38). "He that receiveth a prophet in the name of a prophet shall receive a prophet's reward; and he that receiveth a righteous man in the name of a righteous man shall receive a righteous man's reward" (Matthew 10:41). Those who receive Christ's representatives—his Apostles, his prophets, or his servants the missionaries—have received him, and will be rewarded equally with the Apostles and prophets in his eternal kingdom.

This doctrine is unchanging; thus in our day we hear the Lord saying: "Whosoever receiveth my word receiveth me, and whosoever receiveth me, receiveth those, the First Presidency, whom I have sent" (D&C 112:20). Of the priesthood, which is the power and authority to act for God, the Lord has said: "All they who receive this priesthood receive me . . . ; For he that receiveth my servants receiveth me; And he that receiveth me receiveth my Father; And he that receiveth my Father receiveth my Father's kingdom; therefore all that my Father hath shall be given unto him." (D&C 84:35–38.) By honoring his priesthood and accepting his living servants, we become the rightful heirs of all the blessings promised to the ancient Saints, the same blessings promised prophets and righteous men, the same blessings that embrace the fulness of all that the Father has.

Conversely, the Lord told his disciples that "he that despiseth you despiseth me; and he that despiseth me despiseth him that sent me" (Luke 10:16). Thus, to reject Joseph Smith, to whom the Lord restored his priesthood and its keys and whom he commissioned to teach and testify of him, is the modern equivalent of rejecting the authority, teaching, and testimony of Peter or James or John or even Christ himself. And what is true of Joseph Smith is true of each of his lawful successors in the restored kingdom of God. To reject them is to reject the society and blessings promised to prophets and righteous Saints of all ages—it is to reject the blessings of salvation and the fulness of the Father.

Conclusion

Every argument that can be made against Joseph Smith can be made against Jesus Christ. To oppose those who come in the name of Christ is to oppose Christ. Similarly, every argument that is made against the Book of Mormon can be made against the Bible. If it successfully opposes the Book of Mormon, it will be equally damaging to the Bible or any other manifestation from heaven. As Brigham Young said, "If one be true, both are; and if one be false, both are false."[7] If Jesus is the Christ, then Joseph Smith is a prophet of God, for in all things he taught and testified of Christ.

The spirit that opposes Christ, his gospel, or his prophets is always the same. Again we say that there is no originality in hell. To know the arguments used against Adam, Enoch, Noah, Abraham, Moses, or Christ himself is to know the arguments that are used against Joseph Smith and the Church he restored. The battlegrounds may be new, but the war is not.

CHAPTER 3

The Pharisees and the Signs of the Times

Clothed in the robes of piety and filled with a zeal born of corruption, the religious teachers in the meridian of time closed the heavens, sealed the scriptural canon, corrupted saving ordinances, rejected the everlasting covenant, and sought the blood of the Lord and his servants. The spirit of bitterness and animosity so prevalent in the Savior's day is alive and well in the fulness of times.

Jesus and the Pharisees

Our day is not unlike a time almost two thousand years ago. There is nothing so unsettling to the unillumined intellect and the sterile soul than change. Indeed, spiritual inertia is and has been the malady of millennia, a disease which feeds upon ignorance and is spread most effectively among the complacent. Jesus Christ came to the earth at a time of unrest, an era when men's hearts were closed to a new revelation. Our Lord would, as Isaiah had prophesied some seven hundred years before, grow up "as a root out of a dry ground" (Isaiah 53:2). The parched soil of first century Judaism was deeply in need of living water, but few there were who would dip even the tip of their fingers in the cooling draught to soothe their agonizing thirst; indeed, some were not even aware of the drought.

The Pharisees were a Jewish sect with origins long before the birth of Jesus, about 200 B.C. Their name was probably derived from the Hebrew word *Parash*, meaning "to separate" or "to distinguish." Their desire was to distinguish themselves, to separate themselves regarding their observance of the laws of ritual purity laid down in the traditions of the elders, the particulars of which had been debated for centuries. They were what might be called the "people's party," for Pharisaism was the most popular of the religious sects of the day—one with which over six thousand Jews were aligned in the days of Herod the Great.

Jesus was in constant confrontation with the Pharisees. He attacked their hypocrisy associated with purity of ritual action but paucity of moral and spiritual values. He spoke vehemently against those who zealously attended to rabbinic tradition—matters with little eternal significance—and, at the same time, ignored or violated the "weightier matters of the law, judgment, mercy, and faith" (Matthew 23:23). He condemned the Pharisees further for the irony of their position towards the scriptures: they accepted the oral interpretations and commentaries of the doctors of the law, but refused the healing services of the Great Physician, the one toward whom all the scriptures pointed. "Ye know not Moses, neither the prophets," the Master declared, "for if ye had known them, ye would have believed on me; for to this intent they were written. For I am sent that ye might have life." (JST, Luke 14:36.) Ironically, then, the canon of scripture was open for rabbinic interpretation, but closed to him who came as the fulfillment and extension of the Old Testament.

On one occasion the Pharisees came to Jesus demanding a sign—a physical evidence of his claim to the Messiahship (see Matthew 16:1–4). The Lord took this opportunity to contrast their ability to read the face of the sky (and thus to discern "signs" associated with weather patterns) with their marked inability to read the "signs of the times" (and thus discern the true meanings of Messianic prophecies and testimonies). Soon thereafter Christ warned his disciples: "Take heed and beware of the leaven of the Pharisees and of the Sadducees" (Matthew 16:6). The disciples finally came to appreciate that the Lord was bidding them to beware of the *doctrine*, as well as the *hypocrisy*, of the Jewish leaders. (See Matthew 16:5–12; Luke 12:1.)

The Savior's rejection of hallowed rabbinic traditions, his growing popularity as a result of opening eyes and minds, and his attack upon the heart and hearth of the Pharisaic craft —all these things eventually led to his arrest and death. But the well had been dug, living water had begun to spring up, thirsty souls had been satisfied, and a spiritual foothold had been established for the meridian day.

The Leaven of the Modern Pharisees

Growth, expansion, innovation, and technology have led to remarkable changes in the world over the past two thousand years. On the other hand, some things never change. Religionists without revelation continue to reject living oracles and hold tenaciously to the spiritual status quo. Preachers of a way of life barren of that animation which is breathed into religious practice by the Holy Ghost still seal the canon, thus applying the mortar that blocks the light of new truth and ultimately seals their doom and that of their followers. Congregations still separate themselves from their fellows, claiming to have been reborn or saved, and thus cry out: "We have enough! There is no need for more revelation!'' The challenge of the true believer in all ages is the same: whether former-day Saint or Latter-day Saint, we encounter a world opposed to that change and way of life associated with embracing the new yet everlasting covenant.

The leaven of modern Pharisees is of the same making and substance as that of which the Savior warned. Modern Saints and honest truth-seekers in general must take heed and beware of the corrupting influences of the doctrine and hypocrisy of those bent upon our destruction. Is it not an odd thing to observe a charismatic religious world—people who claim to prophesy and speak in tongues—which rejects the notion of modern Apostles and prophets? Is it not strange that religious leaders across the world—persons who preach of a God interested and involved in human concerns—would warn their patrons against kneeling in prayer to ascertain the truthfulness of the message and claims of Latter-day Saint missionaries and members? Had not Nephi taught his people anciently: "If ye would hearken unto the Spirit which teacheth a man to pray ye would know that ye must pray; for the evil spirit teacheth not a man to pray, but teacheth him that he must not pray''? (2 Nephi 32:8.) Is it not perplexing and tragic that so many outside the Church—those who believe God to be their Father and Jesus Christ to be their pattern for living—in the words of Elder Boyd K. Packer, should "with the help of clergymen, belittle in the most unchristian ways our teaching that we are the literal sons and daughters of God''?[1] These practices and myriad other attitudes reveal clearly that the spirit of Pharisaic hypocrisy is flourishing in the dispensation of the fulness of times. Individuals and congregations will go to any length—including inconsistency, contradiction, or conduct unbecoming a follower of the Prince of Peace—to oppose or halt the progress of a modern revelation of truth.

Doctrine not tied to the pipeline of living oracles will neither be understood nor properly applied. Without such illuminating lenses as the Book of Mormon, the Doctrine and

Covenants, the Joseph Smith Translation, the Pearl of Great Price, and words of modern Church leaders, the Bible has been, and will be forever, a sealed book. Its doctrines and principles will always be wrested and wrestled over. The message of Christ given anciently to the doctors of the law has remarkable modern application: "Woe unto you, lawyers! *For ye have taken away the key of knowledge, the fullness of the scriptures;* ye enter not in yourselves into the kingdom; and those who were entering in, ye hindered." (JST, Luke 11:53; emphasis added.) To deny the Restoration is to deny access to that Spirit by which the will, mind, word, and voice of the Lord (in other words, scripture) is given and comprehended (see D&C 68:3–4). To accept the Restoration and the servants of the Lord is to become open to the mysteries of the kingdom of God—those things which the world will not and cannot receive. These marvelous truths shall, to the sincere seeker, serve as "a well of living water, springing up unto everlasting life" (D&C 63:23).

Reading the Signs of the Times

As noted earlier, the greatest evidence that the Jews in Jesus' day could not read the vital signs of eternity is the simple fact that they missed the Messiah when he came among them. The Hope of Ages had arrived and was ignored or rejected, and those who thus spurned the Lord of Life were left hopeless.

In our day the greatest evidence of people's inability to read and discern the signs of the times is their failure to accept The Church of Jesus Christ of Latter-day Saints as the predicted kingdom of God on earth. In 1981 Elder Bruce R. McConkie asked the following questions of the religious world:

> If you had lived in Jerusalem in the days of Jesus, would you have accepted him as the Son of God as did Peter and the Apostles? Or would you have said he had a devil and wrought

miracles by the power of Beelzebub, as Annas and Caiaphas claimed?

If you had lived in Nazareth or Cana or Capernaum, would you have believed the new religion preached by a few simple fishermen? Or would you have followed the traditions of your fathers in which there was no salvation?

If you had lived in Corinth or Ephesus or Rome, would you have believed the strange new gospel preached by Paul? Or would you have put your trust in the vagaries and traditions and forms of worship that then prevailed?

If you now live in New York or London or Paris, if you live in Chicago, Los Angeles, or Salt Lake—will you accept the new yet old religion, the new yet old gospel, the new yet old way of life that God has revealed anew for our day? Or will you sustain and support churches that no longer have any real resemblance to the one set up among the primitive Saints?

If you hear a prophetic voice, if an apostolic witness is borne in your presence, if the servants of the Lord give you a message from their Master—what is your reaction? Do you believe or disbelieve?

If you are told in words of soberness that Joseph Smith was called of God, that through him the fulness of the everlasting gospel has been restored, and that the Lord has established his church once again among men—do you believe the heaven-sent word? Or, like Annas and Caiaphas, do you stay with the status quo and trust your eternal salvation to the varying forms of man-made worship that abound on every hand?

After bearing witness of the Restoration, Elder McConkie continued:

> Now, as Isaiah expressed it, "Who hath believed our report? and to whom is the arm of the Lord revealed?" (Isaiah 53:1.)
>
> Who will believe our words, and who will hear our message? Who will honor the name of Joseph Smith and accept the gospel restored through his instrumentality?
>
> We answer: the same people who would have believed the words of the Lord Jesus and the ancient Apostles and prophets had they lived in their day.
>
> If you believe the words of Joseph Smith, you would have believed what Jesus and the ancients said.
>
> If you reject Joseph Smith and his message, you would have rejected Peter and Paul and their message.

If you accept the prophets whom the Lord sends in your day, you also accept that Lord who sent them.

If you reject the restored gospel and find fault with the plan of salvation taught by those whom God hath sent in these last days, you would have rejected those same teachings as they fell from the lips of the prophets and Apostles of old. [2]

Reading the signs of the times enables one to not only recognize and adjust to the events of the present, but also to foresee coming events. Those outside the Church who reject its teachings and doctrines are not in a position to perceive and properly adapt to the present and future social, economic, and spiritual challenges. Even those within the Church who have not been wise and thus taken the Holy Spirit for their guide (see D&C 45:57) lack the spirit of discernment and fail to sense the urgency of the messages of the Lord's servants concerning both current and future happenings.

To read the signs of the times is to perceive the unfolding of God's divine drama in these last days—it is to have the total perspective of the plan of life and salvation, and a special appreciation for the scenes incident to its consummation. It is to understand that this is the day long awaited by the prophets of old and by the messengers of heaven, when God would pour out knowledge and power from on high "by the unspeakable gift of the Holy Ghost," knowledge "that has not been revealed since the world was until now" (D&C 121:26).

On the other hand, to read the signs of the times in our day is to read the signs of wear and tear in the faces of those who have chosen to love and give devoted service to either questionable or diabolical causes. Error and wickedness take their terrible tolls upon the hearts and countenances of those who choose divergent paths; the wheels of waywardness grind away slowly but inexorably to produce a type of demented character that will never know peace of mind. To read the signs of the times is, in part, to recognize that Alma spoke a profound truth when he counseled a sinful son that "wickedness never was happiness" (Alma 41:10).

To read the signs of the times in our day does not mean seeking signs in our day. The Savior taught that a wicked and adulterous generation may be recognized by its tendency to demand signs as evidence of the verity of the Lord's work (see Matthew 12:39; 16:4). Interestingly enough, those who are not spiritually mature enough to read the signs of the times are often those who demand signs of the Lord's servants. "Show us the golden plates," they cry out. "Call down the angel Moroni. Furnish the text for the Book of Abraham." The Saints of God who truly seek to be in tune with the mind and will of God will, on the other hand, be witnesses and recipients of those wonders and miracles which a gracious Lord always showers upon his faithful flock. "Faith cometh not by signs," Christ explained in a revelation to Joseph Smith in 1831, "but signs follow those that believe." Continuing: "Without faith no man pleaseth God; and with whom God is angry he is not well pleased; wherefore, unto such he showeth no signs, only in wrath unto their condemnation." (D&C 63:9, 11.)

Finally, to read the signs of the times in our day is to make a decision in favor of the society of Zion and the Church of the Lamb of God (see 1 Nephi 14:10)—this in contrast to a decision to enter or perpetuate Babylon. Each city—Zion and Babylon—makes definite requirements of its citizens, and as the time approaches the millennial day each of these communities will insist upon the total devotion and consecration of its citizenry. To read the signs of the times is to recognize that in the future fewer and fewer individuals will be "lukewarm" Latter-day Saints; that the myopic and misguided of the religious world will grow in cynicism and confusion; that the ungodly will, as time goes by, sink ever deeper into a despair known only to those who revel in iniquity; that wickedness will widen and malevolence multiply until the citizens of Babylon seal themselves to him who is the father of all lies.

To read the signs of the times is to also become aware that "Zion must arise and put on her beautiful garments" (D&C 82:14); that the Church of the Lamb shall continue to require the tithes, offerings, and donations of its members until that day when a full and consecrated life is required; and that through giving all to the Lord through his Church, the Saints of the Most High shall establish a heaven on earth and eventually receive the glorious assurance of exaltation in the highest heaven.

The Closed Canon

The Babylonian Talmud records an anecdote which, though perhaps humorous to us, graphically demonstrates the high and holy station of the Torah among the Jews of an earlier period. It seems that a Rabbi Eliezer was debating with a number of his colleagues.

> Tradition has it that on that day Rabbi Eliezer advanced every conceivable argument without persuading his followers.
> Whereupon he said to them, "If the law be according to my opinion, then let yon carob tree prove it." And a carob tree moved one hundred cubits from its place!
> To which they responded, "What sort of demonstration does a carob tree afford?"
> Whereupon he said to them a second time, "If the law be according to my opinion, let yon stream prove it." And the stream flowed backward!
> To which they responded, "What sort of demonstration does a stream afford?"
> Whereupon he said to them, "If the law be according to my opinion, let the walls of this academy prove it."
> And the walls bent to the point of falling until Rabbi Joshua rebuked them saying, "When scholars contend with one another, what business have ye among them?"
> And so they did not fall out of respect for Rabbi Joshua, and

they did not straighten out of respect for Rabbi Eliezer but remain slanting to this day.

Whereupon Rabbi Eliezer persisted and said to them, "If the law be according to my opinion, let them prove it from on high."

And a heavenly voice sounded forth and said, "What have ye against Rabbi Eliezer after whose opinion the law is always to be framed?"

At which Rabbi Joshua arose and said, "The Torah declares concerning itself, 'It is not up in heaven'; that is to say, *once the Torah was given on Mount Sinai, we pay no heed to heavenly voices* but, as the Torah ordains further, we follow the opinion of the majority.[3]

We see clearly in this entertaining but insightful account the consequence of an unnatural (and certainly unnecessary) attempt to fix and codify the sacred word. In the days of Jesus, it appears that certain Jewish leaders had reached such a point of spiritual sterility that they doubted that God would speak again (see JST, Matthew 7:12–17; compare 1 Nephi 15:8–9), and in some cases even doubted whether there was a God (see JST, Luke 16:20–21).[4] Those who focus too heavily upon what was *once* said (to the exclusion of what is *being* said by one in authority) may look beyond the mark and eventually trade plainness for blindness (see Jacob 4:14).

Pharisees of two thousand years ago rejected Jesus because he represented and proposed an extension to the Old Testament. Pharisees of this last dispensation reject Mormonism because it stands as a supplement, an addendum to what many perceive to be a perfect, complete, and inerrant Bible. (This matter of "Bible worship" will be discussed in more detail in the next chapter. For the time being we should note that in many cases ancient scripture is largely a *history* of religion, and not religion itself.) We cannot rely solely on the thunderings of Sinai or even on the sublime utterances of the Sermon on the Mount; we are desperately in need of our Palmyras, our Kirtlands, our Nauvoos, and our Salt Lake Cities—living fruit from the living tree of life. In a letter to his uncle, Silas Smith, Joseph Smith wrote in 1833 that "the Lord has never given the world to understand, by anything heretofore revealed, that he had ceased forever to speak to his creatures, when sought unto in a proper manner." "Why," the Prophet then asked, "should it be thought a thing incredible that he should be pleased to speak again in these last days for their salvation?"[5]

One of the most vigorous attacks against the Book of Mormon comes in the form of insisting that it replaces or destroys the Bible. Just as Jesus could declare anciently that he had not come to destroy but to fulfill the Law (see Matthew 5:17), even so Latter-day Saints proclaim that the Book of Mormon and the entire Restoration are not sent to undo or lessen all that the prophets of ages past have given. "One of the grand fundamental principles of 'Mormonism,'" said Joseph the Prophet, "is to receive truth, let it come from whence it may."[6] The Prophet also gave this touching and instructive insight into his purpose: "I have no enemies but for the truth's sake. I have no desire but to do all men good. I feel to pray for all men. *We don't ask any people to throw away any good they have got; we only ask them to come and get more.* What if all the world should embrace this Gospel? They would then see eye to eye, and the blessings of God would be poured out upon the people, which is the desire of my whole soul."[7]

After having spoken at length concerning the importance of the Book of Mormon, the Lord said to Joseph Smith in 1828: "And now, behold, according to their faith in their prayers will I bring this part of my gospel to the knowledge of my people. Behold, I do not bring it to destroy that which they have received, but to build it up." Further: "Yea, and I will also bring to light my gospel which was ministered unto them, and, behold, they shall not deny that which you have received, but they shall build it up, and shall bring to light the true points of my doctrine, yea, and the only doctrine which is in me." (D&C 10:52, 62.)

Elder McConkie offered the following poetic counsel, which is appropriate to our subject under consideration:

> We be Abraham's children, the Jews said to Jove;
> We shall follow our Father, inherit his trove.
> But from Jesus our Lord, came the stinging rebuke:
> Ye are children of him, whom ye list to obey;
> Were ye Abraham's seed, ye would walk in his path,
> And escape the strong chains of the father of wrath.
>
> We have Moses the seer, and the prophets of old;
> All their words we shall treasure as silver and gold.
> But from Jesus our Lord, came the sobering voice:
> If to Moses ye turn, then give heed to his word;
> Only then can ye hope for rewards of great worth,
> For he spake of my coming and labors on earth.
>
> We have Peter and Paul, in their steps let us trod;
> So religionists say, as they worship their God.
> But speaks He who is Lord of the living and dead:
> In the hands of those prophets, those teachers and seers,
> Who abide in your day have I given the keys;
> Unto them ye must turn, the Eternal to please. [8]

Conclusion

It is the height of hypocrisy to be outwardly observant and religious, and at the same time closed and opposed to spiritual verities. In short, one is not religious who rejects divinely sent theological truths. One of the prominent Book of Mormon themes is a warning to latter-day readers to deny not the revelations of God. In chapter 28 of 2 Nephi, the prophet Nephi describes evil actions and attitudes of the last days. He speaks of churches being built up, but not to the Lord (v. 3); of priests and ministers teaching with their learning, but denying the Holy Ghost (v. 4); of persons denying the reality and relevance of the Savior (vv. 5—6); of casual and uncaring attitudes—"eat, drink, and be merry, for tomorrow we die" (vv. 7—8); of pride and vainness and false doctrines (vv. 9—14); and of the pathetic pronouncement of those who are "at ease" that "all is well in Zion"

(vv. 20–25). And then, as though Nephi were saving the most horrid and abominable attitude for last, he warns: "Yea, wo be unto him that hearkeneth unto the precepts of men, and denieth the power of God, and the gift of the Holy Ghost! Yea, *wo be unto him that saith: We have received, and we need no more!*" (Vv. 26–27; emphasis added.) The subject is so important to Nephi, and the attitude so deadly, that he devotes approximately twenty more verses to the matter, including that poignant sermon that we read in 2 Nephi 29. To those of our day who have become content with an ancient scriptural record, the Lord gives timeless counsel: "Wherefore, because that ye have a Bible ye need not suppose that it contains all my words; neither need ye suppose that I have not caused more to be written"9 (2 Nephi 29:10).

"It is the constitutional disposition of mankind," Joseph Smith observed, "to set up stakes and set bounds to the works and ways of the Almighty." Of this tendency the Prophet taught: "I say to all those who are disposed to set up stakes for the Almighty, You will come short of the glory of God."10 In light of this principle, and by way of conclusion, let us consider a parable, the application of which is equally relevant to members and nonmembers of the restored Church. Hear now the parable of the hidden treasure.

> The kingdom of heaven is like unto a man who learned of pearls of great price buried in a field. With joy and anticipation he began his search for the precious gems. After barely breaking the surface of the ground he came upon a valuable stone, one which later brought substantial material gain. The man led his friends to the field, and other stones of like worth were uncovered, all barely beneath the surface of the ground. Indeed, as oft as a person chose to drop his trowel or hand spade into the now well-furrowed field, he was almost assured of a valuable find.
>
> And then one day a certain man came to the field alone, a man who had previously uncovered many valuable stones. As he sank his shovel into the earth and pushed beneath

the accustomed level of digging, he happened upon a larger variety of stones and many gems of even greater value. Upon being told of his discovery, many were heard to say: "We have enough! Are these our stones not of great worth? Are they not to be had through digging near the surface?" A few of his friends, however, joyed with him in his prize, and sought the same with eagerness. These persons dug deeper, made similar finds, and were richly rewarded.

Verily, verily, I say unto you, blessed is that man who seeketh deep to find and know the word of God: unto him is given the greater portion of the word, until it is given unto him to know the mysteries of God in full.

CHAPTER 4

The Bible Fraud

The Bible is the most misused and misunderstood book ever
written. It has been used to justify all manner of impropriety,
wickedness, and falsehood. Every spiritual fraud ever per-
petrated in the history of Judaism or Christianity has claimed
support from the Bible. On the authority of the Bible the Jews
crucified Christ, stoned Stephen, and imprisoned and beat
the Apostles. With the Bible as justification Paul persecuted
Christians "unto the death, binding and delivering into
prisons both men and women" (Acts 22:4). After the death of
the Apostles the Bible was taught by the authority of the whip
and the sword. To the Reformers it became the source of
priesthood authority and the final will and testament of their
mute God.

A knowledge of what the Bible does and does not claim for
itself is important in protecting against its misrepresentations
and misuse. Let us consider six common frauds perpetuated
in the guise of loyalty to the Bible.

The Bible Is Not Infallible

The fundamental error of Bible cultists is the doctrine of Bible infallibility. This tenet holds that the Bible must be "completely authoritative and trustworthy in all that it asserts as factual, whether in matters of theology, history, or science."[1] The Bible, it is held, "does not contain error of any kind."[2]

It has to be significant that the Bible makes no such claim for itself! There is not a single passage of scripture that can properly be used to sustain such a view. Nor is there any agreement among those maintaining such a position as to what version of the Bible should be used or what the Bible is saying on a host of matters.

The argument simply is that if the Bible cannot be trusted in all things it cannot be trusted. Because of the nearly endless textual and translation problems, many of our bibliolaters concede errors in our modern Bible while maintaining the infallibility of the original manuscripts as written by their authors. The position is secure since none of the original manuscripts exist and no one would have to accept them as such even if they were found. Still there has to be some question as to the value of a perfect manuscript that doesn't exist. We concede its value to be at least that of a marvelous painting that doesn't exist. It is just difficult to know where to hang it.

It is helpful to ask why the fundamentalists in the Protestant world find it so necessary to argue for an infallible Bible. The answer is that the Bible is all they have. They have no living prophets, they have sealed the heavens to revelation, and even if they were to find some ancient manuscript written by one of the New Testament writers, they have locked themselves into a position that would prevent them from adding it to the canon of scripture. Because the Bible is all they have, it becomes the source of their authority: from it they claim priesthood, doctrine, and the commission to preach and teach. Without it they have nothing. It is a bit like Samson fighting the Philistines with the jawbone of an ass. If it is all you have you use it, but you ought to realize that it is not the ultimate weapon. The ultimate weapon is the power of God that enabled Samson to wield his weapon so effectively. It is that power that we seek, not a modern version of the jawbone (or even the original).

Stone, leaves, bark, skins, wood, metals, baked clay, potsherds, and papyrus were all used anciently to record inspired messages. Our concern with the ancients is not the perfection with which such messages were recorded but with the inspiration of the message. More importantly, we are interested in the fact that the heavens were open to them, that they had such messages to record. Knowing as we do that God is the same yesterday, today, and forever, the fact that he spoke to them, however poorly they preserved it, witnesses that he can speak to us. After all, the Bible is only black ink on white paper until the Spirit of God manifests its true meaning to us; if we have obtained that, what need do we have to quibble over the Bible's suitability as a history and science text?

Three scriptural references are frequently offered to sustain the idea of Bible infallibility: 2 Timothy 3:16; Revelation 22:18–19; and 2 Peter 1:20–21. Let us briefly examine each.

2 Timothy 3:16. "All scripture," wrote Paul, "is given by inspiration of God, and is profitable for doctrine, for reproof, for correction, for instruction in righteousness." This passage is a sentence fragment. If we pursue it to the end of the sentence we read that "all scripture" has been given "that the man of God may be perfect, throughly furnished unto all good works" (v. 17). This emphasis of all good doctrine or scripture being manifest in "good works" might make the passage less popular among those so often quoting it. Yet our concern is its greater context among the revelations of the ancients. Certainly we would agree that "all scripture" inspires, teaches correct doctrine, and is profitable for reproof, correction, and instruction in righteousness. The issue here, however, is what scriptural records Paul had in mind when he made the statement. Was he thinking of the thirty-nine books that make up the Old Testament of the Protestant Bible? or was he thinking of those books plus the fifteen intertestamental books of the Catholic Bible? or did he only have in mind the five books of the Sadducee and Samaritan Bible? or was he thinking of the Jewish Bible, the canon of which (like that of the Christian Bible) was unfixed at that time? We must remember that the scriptural records at Paul's time were written on separate scrolls and that there had not yet been any universal agreement on what was scriptural and what was not. We should also remember that the New Testament had not yet been compiled, indeed the probability is that none of the Gospels had even been written. Now, if Paul was speaking of the infallibility of scriptural records yet to be written, we would certainly want to include in their number the Doctrine and Covenants and the Joseph Smith story, among others.

From the context in which Paul wrote, it is obvious that he is not intending any comment on the infallibility of scriptural records but is commending to his young reader the importance of being a student of the scriptures. Nor is it without significance that the verse itself is mistranslated and ought to read: "And all scripture given by inspiration of God, is profitable for doctrine, for reproof, for correction, for instruction in righteousness" (JST, 2 Timothy 3:16).

Revelation 22:18–19. "For I testify unto every man that heareth the words of the prophecy of this book, if any man shall add unto these things, God shall add unto him the plagues that are written in this book: and if any man shall take away from the words of the book of this prophecy, God shall take away his part out of the book of life, and out of the holy city, and from the things which are written in this book." This passage is frequently used as an argument against the Book of Mormon. Its misuse in the argument for infallibility is based on the same fallacy as is the misuse of 2 Timothy 3:16.

don't add to bible

Those who make this argument hope that Bible readers will suppose that with the addition of the book of Revelation, the Bible now became both complete and perfect. In fact, the passage is the classic illustration of just the opposite. The Bible did not exist when John recorded his revelation. Hundreds of years would yet pass before the books we know as the Bible would be bound together in one volume. In fact no member of the Church that Christ organized ever read the New Testament. The apostasy was complete long before its existence. The book of Revelation, the value of which was resisted by many, came very close to being excluded from the New Testament, and in fact was not published with some early translations of the Bible. There is no honest dispute over the matter that when John spoke about adding to or taking from "the words of the book" he had reference to his book only. What is significant here is that he would seal his book in this manner. It evidences his concern that someone might tamper with what he had written. Now we ask, What would cause him that concern if it were not the fact that it commonly happened?

In all their discussion over Bible infallibility, the sectarian world refuse to acknowledge the possibility that someone deliberately and systematically took things from the Bible or added to it. This was John's concern. Well might he have been concerned because God revealed to Nephi that this very thing was going to happen. The Lord also told Moses that the record he wrote would be tampered with (see Moses 1:41), and Nephi was shown in vision that after the writings of Christ's Apostles went forth "in purity" they would come into the hands of a great and abominable church that would "take away from the gospel of the Lamb many parts which are plain and most precious; and also many covenants of the Lord" would they take away. (See 1 Nephi 13:23–29.) Surely it is not too much to suppose that those who have the blood of Saints on their hands might find it within their conscience to tamper with what the Apostles had written.

2 Peter 1:20–21. "Knowing this first, that no prophecy of the scripture is of any private interpretation. For the prophecy came not in old time by the will of man: but holy men of God spake as they were moved by the Holy Ghost." This passage is quoted by those seeking to establish the infallibility of the Bible by asserting that the scriptures have been dictated word for word by the Holy Ghost and thus can contain no error.

The premise is false. It assumes among other things that all revelations are given with equal clarity. The Bible teaches quite the opposite. For instance, when the Lord was rebuking Miriam and Aaron for the rebellion against Moses, he said: "If there be a prophet among you, I the Lord will make myself known unto him in a vision, and will speak unto him in a dream. My servant Moses is not so. . . . With him will I speak mouth to mouth, even apparently, and not in dark speeches; and the similitude of the Lord shall he behold." (Numbers 12:6–8.) Modern translations (both Catholic and Protestant) say that the Lord would speak to Moses "openly," unlike the other prophets to whom he would speak "in riddles" (see New English Bible and The Jerusalem Bible). Introducing a prophecy to Timothy, Paul wrote, "the Spirit speaketh expressly" (1 Timothy 4:1). That is to say, the Spirit in this instance was "express" and very plain, though that is not always the case. Illustrating that not all experiences with the Holy Ghost are the same, Joseph Smith spoke of the "still small voice, which whispereth through and pierceth all things, and often times it maketh my bones to quake while it maketh manifest" (D&C 85:6).

Brigham Young taught us that there is no such thing as a perfect revelation. Illustrating his point he said: "If an angel should come into this congregation, or visit any individual of it, and use the language he uses in heaven, what would we be benefitted? Not any, because we could not understand a word he said. When angels come to visit mortals, they have to condescend to and assume, more or less, the condition of mortals, they have to descend to our capacities in order to communicate with us."[3] The limited capacity and worthiness of man impose a limitation on the purity with which the heavens can communicate with him.

What then is the doctrine of infallibility? It is a clever way of sealing the heavens and denying the spirit of revelation. It is a grand excuse for rejecting living prophets. It is a pious act indeed—first it declares the Bible to be perfect and complete, and then it is a simple thing to say, "We have enough, we need no more." Thus, the curtains are drawn to shield out heaven's light while we sit in the dark and rave over the accounts of how warm and brilliant that light was anciently. How vain the mind of man to suppose that the fulness of heaven's light could be contained within the covers of a book. Do we really suppose that the Bible contains all that God desires to teach his children, that there is no more, and that the light of heaven cannot breathe new and deeper meaning into its verses today as Christ and his Apostles were so inclined to do as they freely paraphrased and added to the meaning of the Old Testament books in their time? Would it not be wiser and more modest for us to suggest that not a single verse in the Bible is complete, not a single word is beyond God's power to expand and expound, that there can be levels of meaning and prophecies that are fulfilled in a variety of ways?

In the instance of most revelation, God places the thought in the heart and mind of the prophet, and the prophet assumes the responsibility to clothe it in language. When *revelation* God chooses to speak through a person, that person does not become a mindless instrument, an earthly sound system through which God can voice himself. Rather, that person becomes enlightened and filled with intelligence, or truth. God is to be served with both heart and mind; neither agency nor intellect is surrendered. Personality, experience, vocabulary, literary talent—all find expression in recorded revelations. The word of the Lord as spoken through Isaiah is quite different from the word of the Lord as spoken through Luke, and both are different from that spoken through Mark or

Paul. Joseph Smith and Oliver Cowdery shared many
spiritual experiences, but they did not report them in the
same language. For the most part, what we have in the Bible
is not the precise revelation that was given, but rather a
summary announcement that a revelation had been given.

Not All Scripture Is Equal

We can also dismiss the unfortunate idea that everything
in the scriptures is of equal worth. It is hard to imagine that
the Song of Solomon, even if someone can concoct some
meaningful allegory from it, could be thought of as of equal
value with the Sermon on the Mount. And it is difficult to
suppose that the account of the Levite cutting the dead body
of his wife into twelve pieces and sending them to the tribes of
Israel to arouse their anger against those who killed her is of
the same spiritual merit as the Savior's bread of life discourse.
Even within the Bible we can distinguish between that which
is nice to know and that which we must know, and we can
also set some things aside as being quite unnecessary to
know.

Bible Prophets Were Not Infallible

The nature of prophets is of such concern that we will
devote an entire chapter to it. Let it suffice at this point to
observe that the Bible makes no claim that its prophets were
infallible. James wrote of Elijah, one of the greatest of the Old
Testament prophets, that he was "a man subject to like passions as we are" (James 5:17). Paul corrected Peter (see Gala-
tians 2:11–14), and Peter said of Paul that he wrote things
"hard to be understood" (2 Peter 3:16). Jonah misunderstood his own prophecy (see Jonah 4), and Jeremiah got so
discouraged that he said that the Lord had "deceived" him
and swore that he would speak in the name of the Lord no
more (see Jeremiah 20:7, 9). Noah got drunk (see Genesis
9:21). Balaam had his head turned by the promise of riches
and was destroyed with the wicked (see Numbers 31:8), and

Judas, a member of the Twelve, betrayed the Son of God (see Luke 22:47–48).

Nowhere is this principle more beautifully taught than by Moroni: "Condemn me not because of mine imperfection, neither my father, because of his imperfection, neither them who have written before him; but rather give thanks unto God that he hath made manifest unto you our imperfections, that ye may learn to be more wise than we have been" (Mormon 9:31).

The Bible Does Not Have All the Answers

The Bible makes no pretense of having answers to all questions needing answers. Those who make that claim are again making a claim for the Bible that it refuses to make for itself. The supposition that the Bible has all answers raises more questions than it provides answers for. It leaves us wondering why Christ returned for the forty-day ministry after his resurrection, if what is recorded in the Gospels was sufficient for his Apostles (see Acts 1:3). It raises the question why he promised the companionship of the Holy Ghost as a revelator when he was gone (see John 16:12–14). In fact, the Bible continuously directs its readers to implore the heavens for knowledge and understanding beyond what it contains, and often quotes statements and books that are now lost to it. Further, nowhere does the Bible purport to give its readers either authority or commission to preach the gospel or to perform gospel ordinances. Again, to claim such is to claim from the Bible that which the Bible does not claim for itself.

Notwithstanding the fact that the Bible contains the principles of the gospel, it is not the source to which we as Latter-day Saints properly turn to establish doctrine, determine truth, or claim authority. Were the Bible to disappear from the face of the earth today, along with the knowledge of its contents, we as Latter-day Saints would not lose a single doctrine or an iota of authority. All that we have, though confirmed by the Bible, stands independent of it. The revelations of the Bible were given to another people in another day. We are no more dependent on them for the knowledge of salvation than Jesus was dependent on the Old Testament. He freely quoted from it, he testified of its truthfulness, yet he stood independent of it. He never supposed that it had all necessary answers. He drew from it but he also added to it and then announced himself as the pattern for prophets and their followers in all ages. Had there been no Old Testament he still would have been the Son of God. All that was needed in his day was restored anew in his day, and so it is in ours. There are a host of ancient records that will yet be restored to us. We long for them, yet we know that salvation is not, and never has been, found in scriptural records. If salvation is to be found it will be found in a living Christ and in the living of his gospel, not in the record of what others have done.

This is one of the most important lessons that the Prophet Joseph Smith ever sought to teach us. Of his own struggles to find the truth he said, "The teachers of religion of the different sects understood the same passages of scripture so differently as to destroy all confidence in settling the question by an appeal to the Bible" (JS—H 1:12). It is only when the Bible and Book of Mormon "grow together" that there will be a "confounding of false doctrines and laying down of contentions, and establishing peace" (2 Nephi 3:12). The Book of Mormon was given to prove the Bible true, not the reverse (see D:C 20:8—12).

The Bible Does Not Claim to Be Complete

One of the greatest of Bible frauds is the idea that the canon of scripture is complete and that revelation has ceased. In chapter 6 we will deal with this matter in detail; at this point let us merely observe that nowhere does the Bible announce itself to be complete. One of history's ironies is that the Bible prophecies promising continuous revelation were the cause of its being banned following the death of the Apostles. "Toward the end of the second century, after spiritual gifts and revelation had ceased, a man called Montanus came on the scene denouncing the existing apostasy. He announced himself to be the Advocate promised by the Savior and said that he had come to give them the promised revelation." Eventually the church seemed to solve the problem of dealing with such heretics "by announcing that the revelations of God had been given and that the canon of scripture was closed. From then on, they determined that the Spirit was to be confined to aiding men in understanding and applying what had already been written, but no new revelation was to be given."[4]

Accepting the Bible for What It Is

We have noted that the Bible makes no claim to infallibility, to having been supernaturally dictated letter by letter, to everything in it being of equal worth, to the infallibility of its prophets, to having all necessary answers, or to its being the composite of all revelation. The Bible makes no announcement as to what books are to be contained within it, nor does it contain a definition of what scripture is or give any suggested safeguards or warnings to protect us against grievous mistranslations. We have almost numberless variations of Bible texts, the current New Testament alone being a reconstruction of over five thousand separate texts, no two of which are exactly the same.

The spirit of revelation, not the Bible, was the constitution of the church Christ organized. The life-giving force of that church was the Holy Ghost, not twenty-seven books known to us as the New Testament that were not even agreed upon until the end of the fourth century.

Joseph Smith as an Authority on the Bible

Using the Holy Ghost as his textbook, Joseph Smith gave the world its most perfect translation of the Bible, known to us as the Joseph Smith Translation. Of the thousands of Bible translations known to the world, it alone claims to be a work divinely commissioned. In the work of translation Joseph's source was not the thousands upon thousands of Hebrew and Greek manuscripts with their countless contradictions and errors. Rather, Joseph Smith did that which only a prophet could do: he went back to the original language of the scriptures, the language of the Spirit, the language of revelation. The work stands as a testimony of his prophetic calling.

Save Jesus Christ only, the world has never known a more competent Bible authority than Joseph Smith. A library containing everything the world knows about the Bible would not rival his understanding. It is one thing to read the book and quite another to be personally instructed by its authors. Who among the world's scholars or divines can boast of having stood face to face with Adam, Enoch, Noah, a messenger from Abraham's dispensation, Moses, John the Baptist, Peter, James, and John? While religious leaders were claiming the heavens to be sealed to them, Joseph Smith was being personally tutored by these ancient prophets as they laid their hands on his head to bless him and confer upon him the power, keys, and authority they held. Joseph Smith knew the Bible, he knew its prophets, he knew its message, and he knew its central character—the Lord Jesus Christ, with whom he also stood face to face and by whom he was instructed.

Conclusion

To claim for the Bible what it does not claim for itself is to misuse the Bible. The Bible does not claim to be the constitution of the church, it does not claim to be infallible, nor does it claim to be the answer in all things. What the Bible does claim is that whenever God had a people that he acknowledged as his own he spoke to them through living prophets who then added those words to the canon of scripture. The purpose and spirit of the Bible is to open the heavens, not to seal them.

CHAPTER 5

The Weak and the Simple

In their illusory and fanciful conceptions of a prophet's nature and role, designing theologians have decried the necessity and reality of prophets in modern times. Having a form of godliness, but preferring for doctrines the commandments of men, these have robed themselves in darkness at noon day.

Prophets Without Honor Among Men

To a group of erring and misguided Jews of his day, Jesus said, in essence: "Ye think ye have eternal life; but search the scriptures, for they are they which testify of me." Continuing: "And ye will not come to me, that ye might have life." Our Savior then delivered a brief but poignant pronouncement, one which gives us a possible glimpse into his loneliness among doubting mortals, but also reveals his quiet confidence in a Higher Power: *"I receive not honour from men"* (see John 5:39–41; emphasis added). Our Master was honored of his Father, and that knowledge was sufficient to allow him to face the taunts and temptations, the spitefulness and skepticism of those who chose not to honor the most honorable one who ever graced the earth. Such was the lot of the Savior of mankind. Such is generally the lot of those who are called and sent to minister in his name.

"Is not this the carpenter's son?" skeptics asked in the meridian dispensation (see Matthew 13:55; Mark 6:3). "He's one of us; how could he know so much? He's from Nazareth; how could he possibly be the Messiah?" In Joseph Smith's day the questions varied slightly, but the intent was the same. "I knew him as a boy; he's from Manchester, isn't he? What right does he have to claim a revelation from God?" A major malady in all ages has been the world's inability to accept a prophet among the people, a legal administrator with all the challenges and infirmities of mortal men. The problem is simply one of perspective, a matter of unrealistic and unbending expectation.

Jesus was condemned for eating and drinking with publicans and sinners; surely no Deliverer or Redeemer would lower himself to affiliate with the scourge of society. Joseph Smith was condemned for joking and wrestling and playing with the boys; certainly a prophet is made of more austere stuff! Joseph was certainly a prophet, but he was also a man, and needed moments of release from the heavy burdens of directing the kingdom. One member of the Church remarked:

> It tried some of the pious folks to see [Joseph] play ball with the boys. [The Prophet] then related a story of a certain prophet who was sitting under the shade of a tree amusing himself in some way, when a hunter came along with his bow and arrow, and reproved him. The prophet asked him if he kept his bow strung up all the time. The hunter answered that he did not. The prophet asked why, and he said it would lose its elasticity if he did. The prophet said it was just so with his mind; he did not want it strung up all the time.[1]

One man only has walked the earth without sin; he only never took a backward step or even a slight detour from the strait and narrow path. And yet one of the greatest attacks upon prophets centers around their mortality and imperfections. Our tendency to judge (condemn) or pre-judge a prophet may serve in the end as an unerring guide as to how we ought to be judged (see Matthew 7:1–2). Speaking to the Saints in Nauvoo about some who had been overly critical of the Church and its leaders, Joseph Smith said: "I told them I was but a man, and they must not expect me to be perfect; *if they expected perfection from me, I should expect it from them;* but if they would bear with my infirmities and the infirmities of the brethren, I would likewise bear with their infirmities."[2] God calls prophets and God releases prophets. God alone knows the hearts of his servants, and men and women of the world would do well to remember that through less than perfect receptacles the Lord can bring about his perfect purposes. "I never told you I was perfect," Joseph Smith stated, "but there is no error in the revelations which I have taught. Must I, then, be thrown away as a thing of naught?"[3]

Prophets, Apostles, and leaders of the Church at all levels are human. They are called of God, are prompted and guided in their labors regularly, and enjoy the confidence and assurance that accompany divine approbation. But they are human, and as such make mistakes. "Some general authorities are empowered to do one thing and some another. All are subject to the strict discipline the Lord always imposes on his saints and those who preside over them. The positions they occupy are high and exalted. But the individuals who hold these offices are humble men like their brethren in the Church."[4]

As mortals, prophets and leaders are men and women with imperfections common to all mankind. Further, they have (and certainly are entitled to) their own opinions and prejudices. Spiritually mature Latter-day Saints know this, and opponents to the cause of truth would do well to recognize and accept this. It is not necessary for the mantle of authority associated with presiding offices to dictate every thought and word of one's waking state. Every utterance which falls from the lips of a prophet need not be inspired or inspiring. Joseph Smith spoke of visiting "with a brother and sister from Michigan, who thought that 'a prophet is always a prophet'; but I told them that *a prophet was a prophet only when he was acting as such.*"[5] An interesting story in Mormon history concerns President Brigham Young.

> He said some things on some subjects and they were Brigham Young's ideas and not the Lord's. A classic story in the Church on this point is that he talked in the morning session of Conference and gave a fiery speech on a certain subject; then he came back in the afternoon and said: "This morning you heard what Brigham Young thinks about this subject, and now I would like to tell you what the Lord thinks about it." He reversed himself completely. This is an incident that does not demean or belittle him in any sense. It exalts and ennobles him in the eternal perspective in that he, getting the spirit of inspiration and learning what ought to be presented in effect, getting his errand from the Lord—he was willing to bow to the Lord's will and present that philosophy and that suggested procedure to Israel.[6]

Prophets are men approved of God—what further and greater recommendation do we need? Thanks be to the Almighty that he can utilize imperfect beings, and that these men—molded into vessels of holiness in time—prove such a great benefit to their fellow beings (see Mosiah 7:18). In the words of Lorenzo Snow: "I can fellowship the President of the Church if he does not know everything I know. . . . I saw the . . . imperfections in [Joseph Smith]. . . . I thanked God that he would put upon a man who had those imperfections the power and authority he placed upon him . . . for I knew that I myself had weakness, and I thought there was a chance for me. . . . I thanked God that I saw these imperfections."[7]

How Shall We Judge Them?

How then may prophets be assessed? What are the criteria for judging them? Consider the following:

Obscurity or familiarity. Should prophets be rejected because of their obscurity? Because they are from Nazareth or Vermont or Arizona? Because they are little known or because they have no reputation which precedes them? "The trouble with using obscurity as a test of validity," taught a modern prophet, "is that *God has so often chosen to bring forth his work out of obscurity.* He has even said it would be so (see D&C 1:30). Christianity did not go from Rome to Galilee; it was the other way around. In our day the routing is from Palmyra to Paris, not the reverse."[8]

What of familiarity? How many prophets have been rejected because they *had* been known for years by the people in the area? "The trouble with rejection because of familiarity with the prophet is that the prophets are always somebody's son or somebody's neighbor. They are chosen from among the people, not transported from another planet, dramatic as that would be!"[9]

Appearance. In speaking of the Messiah, Isaiah prophesied: "He hath no form nor comeliness; and when we shall see him, there is no beauty that we should desire him" (Isaiah 53:2). The Christ was not to be known by outward appearance; he and his message would be discerned only by those with spiritually alert eyes. Clearly John the Baptist—attired in camel's hair and dining upon locusts and wild honey—would neither be appealing nor appreciated as one of the greatest prophets ever raised up. Saul of Tarsus—who became Paul, the Apostle to the Gentiles—may have been ignored or overlooked if a seeker after truth had anticipated a powerful presence. Of him his contemporaries said: "His letters . . . are weighty and powerful; but his bodily presence is weak, and his speech contemptible" (2 Corinthians 10:10). Those with eyes of faith and souls attuned to the infinite are able to view matters—including God's spokesmen—as God himself views them, for "the Lord seeth not as man seeth; for man looketh on the outward appearance, but the Lord looketh on the heart" (1 Samuel 16:7).

Speech. Not all of the Lord's representatives began their ministries as gifted speakers. Moses responded fearfully to Jehovah on Horeb: "O my Lord, I am not eloquent, neither heretofore, nor since thou hast spoken unto thy servant: but I am slow of speech, and of a slow tongue." But to those called of God, as was Moses, the word of assurance comes: "Go, and I will be with thy mouth, and teach thee what thou shalt say" (Exodus 4:10–12).

Following Enoch's call, he bowed himself to the earth and asked: "Why is it that I have found favor in thy sight, and am but a lad, and all the people hate me; for I am slow of speech; wherefore am I thy servant?" But the Lord knew the heart of this stammering youth—liabilities as well as possibilities— and said: "Go forth and do as I have commanded thee, and no man shall pierce thee. Open thy mouth, and it shall be filled, and I will give thee utterance. . . . Behold my Spirit is upon you, wherefore all thy words will I justify." (Moses 6:31–32, 34.) Enoch's spiritual maturation is evident in Moses' vivid description: "And so great was the faith of Enoch that he led the people of God, . . . and all nations feared greatly, so powerful was the word of Enoch, and so great was the power of the language which God had given him" (Moses 7:13; compare JST, Genesis 14:30–32). One who began his labors as a frightened and ill-equipped young man grew—from grace to grace—until he and his entire society were taken from the earth; today the name of the city of Enoch is always associated with transcendent righteousness.

Personal background. Shall we dismiss a prophet or discount his oracles because of his background? What of Moses who came from and was trained in an idolatrous society, and was for a time a part of the leadership of a world power which

enslaved the children of Israel? Will we spurn Horeb and
Sinai because of Egypt? What of Paul the Apostle, one who
was reared a Pharisee; held the cloaks of those who stoned
Stephen; and was, before the Damascus experience, a
dreaded enemy to the Christians and thus to the gospel
cause? The glorious truth echoed in the lives of these noble
Saints (Moses and Paul)—and many others—is simple: The
heavens do forgive, and man thus has the capacity to be
reborn and thereafter rise above his beginnings. God calls
prophets, and God remakes prophets.

Family background. Not infrequently the credibility of a
prophet is called into question because of the conduct or
doings of family members. Is this a valid measure for ascer-
taining the validity of a prophet's mission? We might want to
keep in mind that Abraham, the father of the faithful, surely
spent many mournful days in prayer in behalf of his own
father, Terah, who was caught up in the idolatries of the area
(see Abraham 1:5; 2:5). If the story may be taken literally, the
Old Testament prophet Hosea was married to a woman
named Gomer, a woman whose morals left much to be
desired. Even the Lord Jesus was a part of a family which was
not totally converted to the truth; it may be that some of
Christ's brothers did not join the Church until after the resurrection (see John 7:1–5). Adam and Eve had offspring who
were murderers, as well as other children and grandchildren
who came to love Satan more than God (see Genesis 4:1–8;
Moses 5:12–57).

With all that has been said, how shall we judge Joseph
Smith? Is it in any way fair to apply to him tests and criteria
that are harsher and more severe than might be applied to
biblical prophets, or even to the Lord Jesus Christ himself? In
1842 Joseph explained: "Although I do wrong, I do not the
wrongs that I am charged with doing; the wrong that I do is
through the frailty of human nature, like other men. No man
lives without fault. *Do you think that even Jesus, if He were here,*

would be without fault in your eyes?"[10] Unfortunately, the unrealistic standards under which Joseph Smith and his works
are so often expected to stand, are such that no man—
prophet or God—could qualify as having been sent by the
Almighty.

One illustration will suffice here. One of the most popular
attacks upon Joseph Smith and Mormonism concerns the
Prophet's First Vision and the fact that Joseph dictated four
different accounts of the 1820 theophany. However, "criti-
cisms of Joseph Smith," one Latter-day Saint historian has
observed, "demand consistency in studying the prophets."

> Many Christians accepting Paul comfortably think that their
> sniping at Joseph Smith's first vision has proved it wrong. But
> what appears is a double standard for these critics. Most argu-
> ments against Joseph Smith's first vision detract from Paul's
> Damascus experience with equal force. For instance, Joseph's
> credibility is attacked because he did not describe his first vision
> until a dozen years after it happened. But the first known men-
> tion of the Damascus appearance is in 1 Corinthians 9:1, written
> about two dozen years after it happened. Critics love to dwell on
> supposed inconsistencies in Joseph Smith's spontaneous
> accounts of his first vision. But people normally give shorter
> and longer accounts of a vivid experience that is retold more
> than once. Joseph Smith was cautious about public explana-
> tions of his sacred experiences until the Church grew strong
> and could properly publicize what God had given him. Thus
> his most detailed first vision account came after several others
> —at the time that he began his formal history that he saw as
> one of the key responsibilities of his life. In Paul's case there is
> the parallel. His most detailed account of Christ's call is the last
> recorded mention of several. Thus before Agrippa, Paul related
> how the glorified Savior first prophesied his work among the
> Gentiles; this was told only then because Paul was speaking
> before a Gentile audience (see Acts 26:16–18). Paul and Joseph
> Smith had reasons for delaying full details of their visions until
> the proper time and place.[11]

We might appropriately ask whether one with a mentality
bent upon denying the reality of the First Vision because
details differ in the various accounts, would also be willing

(and eager) to deny the resurrection of Jesus Christ on the basis that the gospel writers cannot get together on whether there were one or two angels attending the tomb! "The important thing," notes Elder Neal A. Maxwell, "is that the tomb was empty, because Jesus had been resurrected! Essence, not tactical detail!"[12] So also with the experience in the Sacred Grove: the Eternal Father did come with his Beloved Son to the young prophet in 1820, a spiritual reality which may only be known as revealed by the Spirit of God following earnest prayer.

A prophet of God is judged and discerned in the same manner as all things of God are received: by the power of the Holy Ghost. This is the supreme test, one which places the burden of proof upon the critic or investigator. Too often those who attack and slander and assign questionable motives are spiritually lethargic, simply too lazy to apply the final litmus test of truth—i.e., they refuse to come to know (through personal worthiness and personal strivings) the truth and divinity of the cause espoused by the Latter-day Saints. So long as the Book of Mormon remains the one book which has the most reviewers but fewest readers, the truth of the work in which we are engaged will never be widely known. So long as persons outside the faith refuse to pray in faith, the waiting witness will not come, worlds without end.

The Preparation of a Prophet

After young Joseph Smith emerged from the Palmyra woods, nothing was quite the same. Joseph knew, and those touched by the power and sincerity of his witness knew, that the heavens were no longer sealed and that God and Christ were living realities. He likewise knew from a dreadful personal encounter that the arch-deceiver was more than mythical. Yes, the fourteen-year-old prophet knew a great deal more following the visit of the Father and Son than learned divines of that day and future days would know after a lifetime of scholarly inquiry. But Joseph did not know everything then, nor did he when he breathed his last breath on a hot and sultry day twenty-four years later. Prophets, like other people, must learn and develop bit by bit, line upon line, knowledge upon knowledge. Even in their prophetic prime they may not know all things. Is this so odd? Should we expect otherwise?

An angel appeared to Nephi to give him a directed tour through his vision of the future. One of the early scenes of the vision was of Mary, the mother of Jesus. The angel then asked: "Knowest thou the condescension of God?" Nephi answered in simple honesty: "I know that he loveth his children; nevertheless, I do not know the meaning of all things" (1 Nephi 11:16–17; see verses 13–17). Nephi's humility evidenced his capability to be instructed in a marvelous manner. About five hundred years later Alma delivered a remarkable address to the people in Gideon, the core of which was a messianic prophecy: "There is one thing which is of more importance than they all—for behold, the time is not far distant that the Redeemer liveth and cometh among his people. Behold, I do not say that he will come among us at the time of his dwelling in his mortal tabernacle; for behold, the Spirit hath not said unto me that this should be the case. Now as to this thing I do not know; but this much I do know, that the Lord God hath power to do all things which are according to his word" (Alma 7:7–8; compare 40:19–20).

Joseph Smith, like all the prophets, required divine care and schooling; he was not the same seer in 1820 that he would prove to be in 1844. The Prophet required occasional chastening in the formative years of the Church. The Lord delivered the following stinging sermon to Joseph in 1828: "Although a man may have many revelations, and have power to do many mighty works, yet if he boasts in his own strength, and sets at naught the counsels of God, and follows after the dictates of his own will and carnal desires, he must fall and incur the vengeance of a just God upon him" (D&C

3:4). Note that there has been no attempt by the Prophet Joseph to cover up the Lord's rebuke; it is plainly in view of all who would sincerely learn lessons from one like Joseph Smith. And yet after a season of refinement—an era of both ghastly and glorious encounters—that same Lord spoke tenderly to his servant in 1843: "I am the Lord thy God, and will be with thee even unto the end of the world, and through all eternity; for verily I seal upon you your exaltation, and prepare a throne for you in the kingdom of my Father, with Abraham your Father" (D&C 132:49).

Joseph Smith, like Moses of old, was not a gifted public speaker during the early years of his ministry. Men like Oliver Cowdery and Sidney Rigdon were of great value to Joseph and the Church, and frequently served as spokesmen for the young and unlearned prophet. (See, for example, D&C 28:3; 100:9.) But with time and tutoring and experience came talent and spiritual gifts; in time, Joseph Smith became a mighty spokesman for the Lord.[13] He became the walking embodiment of scripture, a vessel of light. "I thank God," he said just two months before his death, "that I have got this old book [German Bible]; but I thank him more for the gift of the Holy Ghost. I have got the oldest book in the world; but I [also] have the oldest book in my heart, even the gift of the Holy Ghost."[14] Parley P. Pratt relates the following incident which evidences the role of Joseph Smith as a mature and independent witness of the truth:

> While visiting with brother Joseph in Philadelphia, a very large church was opened for him to preach in, and about three thousand people assembled to hear him. Brother Rigdon spoke first, and dwelt on the Gospel, illustrating his doctrine by the Bible. When he was through, brother Joseph arose like a lion about to roar; and being full of the Holy Ghost, spoke in great power, bearing testimony of the visions he had seen, the ministering of angels which he had enjoyed; and how he had found the plates of the Book of Mormon, and translated them by the gift and power of God. He commenced by saying: "If nobody else had the courage to testify of so glorious a message from

Heaven, and of the finding of so glorious a record, he felt to do
it in justice to the people, and leave the event with God."[15]

A final thought with regard to the preparation of prophets:
Not only does God prepare his prophets and prepare his children to receive the appointed prophets, he further desires
that all men and women follow the prescribed pattern and
become prophets themselves. Ours should be a kingdom of
priests and priestesses, a society of prophets and prophet-
esses. Obviously there is and should be order and direction
in the kingdom of God. One man only holds the keys of revelation for the entire Church. Further, it is indeed contrary to
the order of heaven for one to receive divine direction for
those in positions of authority higher than one's own. And
yet every member of the Church can and should become a
prophet for himself, his family, and those under his direct
care. Joseph Smith was asked in 1838: " 'Do you believe
Joseph Smith, Jun., to be a Prophet?' " He responded: "Yes,
and every other man who has the testimony of Jesus. For *the
testimony of Jesus is the spirit of prophecy.*"[16] (See Revelation
19:10.)

It is not for the chaplain in the military to be the only man
on a military base to concern himself with spiritual or religious matters; such is certainly too often the case, and such
an attitude simply takes from the individuals responsibility
which is unquestionably their own. So also in the kingdom of
God: prophets and Apostles and General Authorities carry an
enormous load in directing the affairs of the world-wide
Church; however, the assignment for spiritual growth, the
obligation to obtain and perfect the witness of the work, and
the responsibility to enjoy the quiet but certain workings of
the Spirit—these matters rest with individual members. An
account described in the Old Testament demonstrates beautifully the desires of God and his prophets in this regard. The
Lord came down among Moses and his people, spoke to
them, and poured out his Spirit upon seventy of the elders of
Israel. Two of the number in the camp, Eldad and Medad,

were moved by the sacred powers present and began to prophesy among the people. Joshua, certainly well-meaning, but perhaps fearful and a bit possessive for Moses' prophetic mantle, cried out: "My lord Moses, forbid them." And then came the provocative and penetrating reply from the lawgiver, an answer which has real relevance in this final dispensation: "Enviest thou for my sake? *Would God that all the Lord's people were prophets, and that the Lord would put his spirit upon them!*" (See Numbers 11:24–29; emphasis added.)

Conclusion

It is a singular privilege to live in a day when prophets and Apostles walk the earth. Today we are immersed in a dispensation of revelation, and we have ready access to eternal truths. We are also a part of an age, conversely, where many in the world have been "blinded by the subtle craftiness of men" (see D&C 76:75), and have come to misunderstand the necessity and nature of prophets. But thanks be to God that we now have modern prophets to reveal the work and wisdom of the Lord, that all the world may learn how and where the truths of salvation may be found.

In this day and time (as well as in times of old) the fulness of the gospel is "proclaimed by the weak and the simple unto the ends of the world, and before kings and rulers" (D&C 1:23). In the words of Elder B. H. Roberts, "Joseph Smith . . . claimed for himself no special sanctity, no faultless life, no perfection of character, no inerrancy for every word spoken by him. And as he did not claim these things for himself, so can they not be claimed for him by others. . . . Yet to Joseph Smith was given access to the mind of Deity, through the revelations of God to him."[17] In our day it is fashionable to stress the humanity and weaknesses of Joseph Smith and his successors; to cast aspersions on their motives or characters; and to reveal historical details, the context and true meanings of which are lacking. Unfortunately, Joseph the Prophet cannot be with us now to answer all charges against him. But be it remembered that the God of heaven has called and approved Joseph Smith and those associated with him; those who attempt to mar the name and image of the Prophet of the Restoration will eventually answer to God himself for their actions. It was President George Albert Smith who observed: "Many have belittled Joseph Smith, but those who have will be forgotten in the remains of mother earth, and the odor of their infamy will ever be with them, but honor, majesty, and fidelity to God, exemplified by Joseph Smith and attached to his name, will never die."[18]

CHAPTER 6

Line Upon Line

As with prophets, so with revelation: the minds of designing men have perpetuated a fraud. It is a fraud born of ignorance of how revelation comes and how it operates upon the hearts and minds of men. The true and living church is always characterized by revelation which grows, expands, and develops. The Spirit manifests itself line upon line, precept upon precept.

The Odyssey of the Living Church

Revelation is the process by which the mind of God is impressed on the mind of man, the means by which—individually and institutionally—the will of the heavens is made known and carried out in the earth. Divine potential cannot be achieved without such communication for "salvation cannot come without revelation; it is in vain for anyone to minister without it."[1]

We live in an odd age, a time when multitudes of people on earth preach and believe that salvation is obtained through receiving the appointed number of church sacraments, and that revelation ceased, for the most part, with the meridian apostolic witnesses. Others are eager to participate in what they perceive to be modern pentecostal outpourings, convinced that institutionally God has not chosen to speak or reveal himself beyond the first century A.D., i.e., beyond the New Testament record of revelation. "The Bible," they protest to the Latter-day Saints, "is our revelation and our authority!" On the one hand, then, myriads of persons hold tenaciously to the traditions and rituals of the Christian churches. Other groups see little necessity for organizational ties, but rather are elated by what they suppose has come into their hearts and transformed their lives. In reality, truth cuts a road between these two extremes. Regarding being born again, for example, Joseph Smith said simply: "Being born again, comes *by the Spirit of God through ordinances.*"[2] Both institutional and individual revelation are necessary if both body and spirit are to be inseparably joined to form the soul of religious practice.

In his Preface to our modern revelations contained in the Doctrine and Covenants, the Lord spoke of the Restoration as a process whereby he might take the Church and "bring it forth out of obscurity and out of darkness; the *only true and living church* upon the face of the whole earth, with which I, the Lord, am well pleased" (D&C 1:30; emphasis added). Testimonies by the legion are borne to the effect that The Church of Jesus Christ of Latter-day Saints is the only *true* church on earth; the Lord's testimony, in addition, is that we belong to the only *living* church upon the face of the earth. The Church is *alive*. It is not dead. It is not dying. It is not even wounded! As a living organism, the Church grows and develops; it responds to external stimuli; it is a kinetic kingdom. The Church organization might be said to be perfect in our day, not in the sense that it is set in stone and is unchanging and established, but rather because it changes and seeks to respond, in inspired fashion, to current trends and modern crises in a way to perfectly meet the members' needs at a given time. Grounded in eternal and unchanging principles, the life of the Church is in part evident in its adaptability. Elder Orson Pratt observed: "To say that there will be a stated time, in the history of this Church, . . . that there will be no further extension or addition to the organization, would be a mistake. Organization is to go on, step after step, from one degree to another, just as the people increase and grow in the knowledge of the principles and laws of the the kingdom of God."[3]

The true Church of Jesus Christ reconciles the irreconcilable. It provides safety and security in the *static* (priestly) dimension of religion, the quiet assurance that one is grounded and settled on the bedrock of a sure foundation of faith. It also offers life and excitement associated with the *dynamic* (prophetic) dimension of religion, the animation and vitality that comes from the continuing influences of the Holy Ghost. The Church of Jesus Christ is static in that it is grounded in the faith of the ancients, and teaches a gospel that was had not only by Peter, James, and John but also by Adam, Seth, and Enos; we are tied theologically to first century Christianity, ancient Israel, and the early patriarchs. The Church of Jesus Christ is dynamic in the sense that it is dependent on current revelation for its daily operation — living fruit from the living tree of life.

We honor and reverence the names and works of those who have gone before. But their revelations are not sufficient to save this generation. In the words of Joseph Smith:

> You will admit that the word spoken to Noah was not sufficient for Abraham or it was not required of Abraham to leave the land of his nativity and seek an inheritance in a strange country upon the word spoken to Noah. But for himself he obtained

promises at the hand of the Lord and walked in that perfection
[so] that he was called the friend of God. Isaac, the promised
seed, was not required to rest his hope upon the promises made
to his father, Abraham, but was privileged with the assurance
of his approbation in the sight of heaven by the direct voice of
the Lord to him. *If one man can live upon the revelations given
to another, might not I with propriety ask why the necessity then of
the Lord speaking to Isaac as he did?* . . .

I have no doubt but that the holy prophets and apostles and
saints in ancient days were saved in the Kingdom of God.
Neither do I doubt but that they held converse and communion
with [the heavens] while in the flesh. . . . I may believe that
Enoch walked with God; I may believe that Abraham com-
muned with God and conversed with angels . . . ; but will all
this purchase an assurance for me, or waft me to the regions of
eternal day with my garments spotless, pure, and white? Or,
must I not rather obtain for myself, by my own faith and diligence in keeping the commandments of the Lord, an assurance
of salvation for myself? And *have I not an equal privilege with
the ancient saints?*[4]

In 1867 President Heber C. Kimball prophesied: "This
Church has before it many close places through which it will
have to pass before the work of God is crowned with victory.
To meet the difficulties that are coming, it will be necessary
for you to have a knowledge of the truth of this work for yourselves. The difficulties will be of such a character that the
man or woman who does not possess this personal knowledge or witness will fall." He further testified: "The time will
come when no man nor woman will be able to endure on
borrowed light. Each will have to be guided by the light
within himself."[5] This light may be borrowed neither from
those of the present nor those of the past; we will not be
saved or spared by God's revelations to biblical prophets
anymore than we will by his revelation to another person in
our own day. We may be saved no more by someone else's
revelation than we can be by their repentance, baptism, and
witness of the Spirit. Individual and institutional direction
from God must be current and alive.

The Nature of Prophecy

Prophecy is one of the marvelous gifts of the Spirit, one of the many signs and wonders that always accompany the fulness of the gospel, the living Church, and those Saints that believe. It is one means by which regenerated man may gain God's objective perspective and thus "have great views of that which is to come" (Mosiah 5:3). Some prophecies are unconditional and will come to pass regardless of circumstances or events. For example, the coming of Jesus Christ into the world was prophesied millennia before the event was to occur. Prophets and wise men and women recognized that the Redeemer would come in the meridian of time, regardless of the people's worthiness or readiness. We certainly have no prophetic utterance on record wherein the people were told that if they would repent (or would *not* repent) the Messiah would come. It is just so with the Savior's second coming: the precise time of that "great and dreadful day," though unknown to the Saints and the world, is set and established.[6]

Prophecies may also be of a conditional nature. In other words, if *A* takes place, then *B* will come to pass. The Book of Mormon provides one of our best illustrations of such a prophecy. "Inasmuch as ye shall keep my commandments [note the condition]," the Lord explained to the Nephites, "ye shall prosper in the land; but inasmuch as ye will not keep my commandments ye shall be cut off from my presence" (2 Nephi 1:20). A patriarchal blessing also represents a conditional prophetic utterance—the blessings and privileges promised therein are contingent upon the faithfulness of the recipient.

Sometimes prophecies are not fulfilled because of circumstances outside the control of the one to whom the divine word was spoken. In 1832 the Lord spoke through the Prophet Joseph Smith: "Verily this is the word of the Lord, that the city New Jerusalem shall be built by the gathering of the saints, beginning at this place [Independence, Missouri], even the place of the temple, which temple shall be reared in this generation. For verily this generation shall not all pass away until an house shall be built unto the Lord." (D&C 84:4–5.) Critics of the Church, and particularly those who desire to cast doubt upon the divine call of the Prophet, are eager to emphasize that a temple certainly was *not* constructed in Jackson County during the lifetime of the Prophet; they are quick to add that the predicted temple still has not been erected.

In a later revelation given to the Prophet in Nauvoo, however, the Lord explained: "Verily, verily, I say unto you, that when I give a commandment to any of the sons of men to do a work unto my name, and those sons of men go with all their might and with all they have to perform that work, and cease not their diligence, *and their enemies come upon them and hinder them* from performing that work, behold, it behooveth me to require that work no more at the hands of those sons of men, but to accept of their offerings" (D&C 124:49; emphasis added). In this case enemies to the Church prevented the immediate fulfillment of the 1832 prophecy.

Those who understand the conditional nature of most prophecy will not be shaken when they encounter unfulfilled prophecy or change in the Lord's plans. Perhaps the best illustration of the latter principle is found in the ministry of Jonah. Called to preach to the decadent and depraved city of Nineveh (the capital of Assyria), Jonah was instructed: "Arise, go to Nineveh, that great city, and cry against it; for their wickedness is come up before me" (Jonah 1:2). As is widely known, however, Jonah chose to flee from his assignment and "from the presence of the Lord." After a harrowing experience, wherein the prophet became convinced of his inescapable duty, the word of Jehovah came again to a rapidly repentant Jonah: "Arise, go unto Nineveh, that great city, and preach unto it the preaching that I bid thee." This time Jonah obeyed, entered the city, and cried out: "Yet forty days, and Nineveh shall be overthrown." To Jonah's complete surprise, "the people of Nineveh believed God, and proclaimed a fast, and put on sackcloth, from the greatest of them even to the least of them" (Jonah 3:1–5). Destruction was averted through the preaching of a servant of God and the unexpected repentance of a formerly wicked people. Prophecy does not predestinate.

In many cases the members of the Church must simply be patient and exercise faith in the Lord's servants to witness the fulfillment of prophecy. No doubt some of Joseph Smith's prophetic utterances were so unusual or unexpected that many of the early Saints found themselves questioning and doubting. But those who had received the witness of the truth knew that Joseph Smith had been called of God, that his words represented the mind and will of the Lord for the Latter-day Saints, and that it would only be a matter of time before the prophetic pronouncements would be vindicated. President Harold B. Lee reminded us repeatedly that a man or woman is not truly converted until he sees the power of God resting upon the leaders of this Church, and then has that witness go down into his heart and burn like fire.[7] Once that fire is burning, then it is only a matter of trusting those who lead and resting secure in the knowledge that the Lord's purposes will be accomplished according to his divine schedule. At the time of the Church's organization the Lord instructed: "Wherefore, meaning the church, thou shalt give heed unto all his [the President's] words and commandments which he shall give unto you as he receiveth them, walking in all holiness before me; For his word ye shall receive, as if from mine own mouth, *in all patience and faith.*" (D&C 21:4–5; emphasis added.)

Change and Growth

Isaiah warned of a future day of wickedness and of a generation with perverted priorities: "Woe unto them that call evil good, and good evil; that put darkness for light, and light for darkness; that put bitter for sweet, and sweet for bitter!'' (Isaiah 5:20; 2 Nephi 15:20). In our day one of the most prominent attacks on the Church concerns *change:* changing Church practices and policies, changing procedures, changes in revelations, and so on. Odd, isn't it, that what in the eternal perspective bespeaks life and breath in the kingdom of God—i.e., *change*—should be perceived with disdain by those wanting in the spirit of truth! Ironically, the very things that skeptics and critics eschew as obvious flaws and deficiencies prove to be pillars and cornerstones of the faith. Indeed, the ''changing world of Mormonism'' is a world of hope, enthusiasm, and vibrant *life.*

Joseph the Prophet is frequently attacked for altering or adding to that which he had previously written or dictated. ''If the original were given by inspiration of God,'' the critics ask, ''then what further need is there for revisions or addenda?'' The very question shows ignorance of the spirit of revelation. Such misunderstanding would make the Spirit a prisoner, confined within the covers of a single book, and seal the Spirit in a set number of words or expressions. On the other hand, those who are acquainted with the workings of the Spirit of the Lord know full well that in most cases the recipient of a divine directive is not simply a ventriloquist for God, not simply a recording device from which the perfect and inerrant word comes forth. Rather, the idea is conveyed through the Spirit to the receiver's mind, and then, with heavenly assistance, the concept is transformed into language. Joseph Smith made hundreds of revisions in the manuscripts of the Book of Mormon, the Doctrine and Covenants, and his inspired translation of the King James Bible. With regard to revisions in his labors with the Bible, Robert J. Matthews has written:

> In the face of the evidence it can hardly be maintained that the exact words were given to the Prophet in the process of a revelatory experience. Exact words may have been given to the mind of the Prophet on occasion, but the manuscript evi-

dence suggests that generally he was obliged to formulate the words himself to convey the message he desired. Consequently, he might later have observed that sometimes the words were not entirely satisfactory in the initial writings. They may have conveyed too much or too little. Or they may have been too specific or too vague, or even ambiguous. Or the words may have implied meanings not intended. Thus through (1) an error of recording, (2) an increase of knowledge, or (3) an inadequate selection of words, a passage of the New Translation might be subject to later revision.[8]

What was true with regard to the Bible translation was equally true in other areas. For example, in April of 1829 Joseph Smith and Oliver Cowdery received a fascinating revelation concerning the status of John the Beloved. This revelation was published as chapter 6 of the 1833 Book of Commandments. When the Prophet prepared the first edition of the Doctrine and Covenants (1835), he added several verses to the original revelation to complete what we now have as Doctrine and Covenants, section 7. Either through additional revelation (between 1829 and 1835) or increased understanding, Joseph was able to supply a number of details not present in the original document. This is a prophetic-editorial work rightly belonging to the Lord's legal administrators. It is, indeed, the prophetic prerogative to do such things, and those who are offended by such actions are generally those under the yoke of misunderstanding and incorrect ideas.

We would do well to consider an interesting story told in chapter 36 of Jeremiah. It seems that the word of the Lord came to Jeremiah instructing him to record the prophecies concerning the impending Babylonian destruction. Baruch, his faithful scribe, penned the prophetic word and then read the ominous message before the dignitaries of Judah, including the king, Jehoiakim. Jehoiakim and those of a similar mentality saw to it that the bad news was disposed of: the scroll was thrown into the fire and burned. The word of the Lord came again: "Take thee again another roll, and write in

it all the former words that were in the first roll, which
Jehoiakim the king of Judah hath burned" (v. 28). Jeremiah
and Baruch were obedient to the command. And now note
the concluding verse of the chapter: "Then took Jeremiah
another roll, and gave it to Baruch the scribe, . . . who wrote
therein from the mouth of Jeremiah *all the words of the book
which Jehoiakim king of Judah had burned* in the fire: *and there
were added besides unto them many like words"* (v. 32; emphasis
added).

Just as prophets grow line upon line, so it is not unusual
for new truths to come to prophets in like fashion, even
spiritual supplements to what they have already received. A
classic illustration with the Prophet is recorded by Elder
George Reynolds:

> While residing in Kirtland Elder Reynolds Cahoon had a
> son born to him. One day when President Joseph Smith was
> passing his door he called the Prophet in and asked him to bless
> and name the baby. Joseph did so and gave the boy the name
> of Mahonri Moriancumer. When he had finished the blessing
> he laid the child on the bed, and turning to Elder Cahoon he
> said, the name I have given your son is the name of the brother
> of Jared; *the Lord has just shown (or revealed) it to me.* Elder
> William F. Cahoon, who was standing near, heard the prophet
> make this statement to his father; and this was the first time
> the name of the brother of Jared was known in the Church in
> this dispensation. [9]

Joseph Smith had translated the Book of Mormon many years
before, and certainly had become intimately acquainted with
the characters in that record. But a new occasion provided the
impetus for a new revelation.

Some changes and developments take place very gradu-
ally, others quite suddenly. But when changes are divinely
directed, the Saints of God are eager and willing to adapt and
respond appropriately. In the early days of the Restoration,
for example, a person evidenced his discipleship by *gathering.* Gathering was and is a two-fold process: one gathered
first spiritually, by accepting the true Messiah and becoming

a part of the Church and fold of God (see 2 Nephi 9:1–2); and one gathered physically by locating himself where the Saints of God congregated. In the early and mid-nineteenth century new converts longed to gather with the strength of the newly found faith, and thus frequently relocated themselves and their families to the Church's gathering place—be that Ohio or Missouri or Illinois or the Great Salt Lake Valley. By about 1890 the leaders of the Church began to have an expanded vision of the importance of the distant stakes of the "tent of Zion" (see Isaiah 54:2; D&C 82:14). Thereafter new converts were asked to "gather" to their local stakes and to stay in their own lands in order that the expanding tent of Zion might be an even stronger influence worldwide.

In what may be termed a modern doctrinal benchmark regarding the gathering to Zion, Elder Bruce R. McConkie explained to the Saints of Mexico and Central America in August of 1972: "The place of gathering for the Mexican Saints is Mexico; the place of gathering for the Guatemalan Saints is in Guatemala; . . . and so it goes throughout the length and breadth of the whole earth. . . . Every nation is the gathering place for its own people."[10] This is only one example of many that could be cited as evidence of change and growth in the established kingdom of God. The Restoration which began on a beautiful spring morning in 1820 is still underway. Many precious principles are being unveiled each day through the channels established by the Almighty; great and marvelous truths—all a part of the prophesied restitution of all things—will yet be revealed. Change, growth, and development will be integral parts of The Church of Jesus Christ of Latter-day Saints, particularly as we anxiously move toward the anticipated millennial day.

Conclusion

"No man can receive the Holy Ghost," the Prophet Joseph Smith taught, "without receiving revelations. The

Holy Ghost is a revelator."[11] With the Holy Ghost operating on the hearts and minds of its recipients, the people of the Lord can begin to have their vision expanded and their perspective broadened, so as to see things as God sees them — as they really are. In so doing, the elect of God seek to bring things on earth into conformity with that which is in heaven. And thus it is that the living Church is grounded in that preeminent principle on which the government of heaven is conducted — "*revelation adapted to the circumstances in which the children of the kingdom are placed.*"[12] Our scriptural canon is open and flexible; as we learn and live that which has been given already by a gracious Lord, surely more truths will be restored and revealed. And again, what of change? Elder Orson Pratt asked: "Are we then to be governed in all respects by those limited things that we were governed by in our childhood? Will there be no change of circumstances?" And then he answered his own question: Yes, since "new circumstances require new power, new knowledge, new additions, new strength."[13]

CHAPTER 7

Fruits or Roots:
How Shall Ye Know Them?

How are the truths of salvation to be known? In our search for truth ought we to turn to prophets or scholars, temples or universities? Is the environment of the Spirit one of certitude or cynicism, simplicity or complexity, purity or popularity? Is it within the capacity of all to weigh and measure truth or must we depend on the judgment of others? And if we can indeed know for ourselves, can we do so with confidence that we have not been deceived?

Gospel Truths Are Absolute

The truths of salvation are absolute and eternal. They vary not. What is true in one age is true in every age. Were it not so, we could not seek God with confidence. Since God is the same yesterday, today, and forever, all can seek the will of God and the blessings of heaven with the confidence of obtaining them through righteous living. The Spirit and its operations are ever the same. If we know how that Spirit operated anciently we know how that Spirit will operate today; conversely, if we know how it operates today we know how it operated anciently.

The Spirit of God produces the same results and the same testimony in those of all nations and in all ages of earth's history. "Devout men, out of every nation under heaven" heard the testimony of Peter on the day of Pentecost, and each received the same witness, though they spoke a multiplicity of tongues (see Acts 2:5–6). There is no time limitation on the Savior's statement that "if ye are not one ye are not mine" (D&C 38:27). The scriptures tell us that God "imparteth his word by angels unto men, yea, not only men but women also. Now this is not all; little children do have words given unto them many times, which confound the wise and the learned." (Alma 32:23.) All are invited to come to him and partake of his goodness; he denieth none, "black and white, bond and free, male and female; and he remembereth the heathen; and all are alike unto God, both Jew and Gentile" (2 Nephi 26:33).

If all are invited, even commanded, to come to God, can we not reason that all have the innate capacity to recognize and know the truths of salvation? And if all can know, and we are not dependent on universities or trained divines to show the way, then the tests of truth must be universally available and universally manageable. So it ought to be and so it is. None have made this more simple or more direct than the Savior, who gave the test in seven succinct words: "Ye shall know them by their fruits" (Matthew 7:16). Let us consider the test.

Testing the Book of Mormon

Criticism of the Book of Mormon began even before it was published. It has been referred to as the one book that doesn't have to be read to be reviewed. Missionaries by the tens of thousands have heard the Book of Mormon condemned by people who have never read a word of it or heard anyone else do so. All manner of theories have been postulated to explain the book away. It has been widely published that it was plagiarized from a manuscript written by a former Presbyterian minister named Solomon Spaulding; others have argued that since Joseph Smith was not capable of writing it, Sidney Rigdon must have done it; while yet another theory holds that it reflects the genius of Joseph Smith in synthesizing current events in the form of an ancient record. Considerable energy has been expended to avoid actually reading the book. Hugh Nibley captures the ridiculousness of these efforts in a parable of a diamond found in a field.

A young man once long ago claimed he had found a large diamond in his field as he was ploughing. He put the stone on display to the public free of charge, and everyone took sides. A psychologist showed, by citing some famous case studies, that the young man was suffering from a well-known form of delusion. An historian showed that other men have also claimed to have found diamonds in fields and been deceived. A geologist proved that there was no diamonds in the area but only quartz: The young man had been fooled by a quartz. When asked to inspect the stone itself, the geologist declined with a weary, tolerant smile and a kindly shake of the head. An English professor showed that the young man in describing his stone used the very same language that others had used in describing uncut diamonds: he was, therefore, simply speaking the common language of his time. A sociologist showed that only three out of 177 florists' assistants in four major cities believed the stone was genuine. A clergyman wrote a book to show that it was not the young man but someone else who had found the stone.

Finally an indigent jeweler named Snite pointed out that since the stone was still available for examination the answer to the question of whether it was a diamond or not had absolutely nothing to do with who found it, or whether the finder was honest or sane, or who believed him, or whether he would know a diamond from a brick, or whether diamonds had ever been found in fields, or whether people had ever been fooled by quartz or glass, but was to be answered simply and solely by putting the stone to certain well-known tests for diamonds. Experts on diamonds were called in. Some of them declared it genuine. The others made nervous jokes about it and declared that they could not very well jeopardize their dignity and reputations by appearing to take the thing too seriously. To hide the bad impression thus made, someone came out with the theory that the stone was really a synthetic diamond, very skilfully made, but a fake just the same. The objection to this is that the production of a good synthetic diamond 120 years ago would have been an even more remarkable feat than the finding of a real one. [1]

Modern history knows no book more criticized or vehemently damned by priests and clergy than the Book of Mormon. What is of interest is that there has never been a single instance in which these critics of the book have attempted to use the standard given by the Savior to discern truth from error. Never has one of these so-called spiritual leaders stood before their congregations or suggested to those to whom they wrote that they apply the simple test suggested by the book itself—read it and pray about it. On the contrary, countless efforts have been made to discredit the book through the use of bad history or poor reasoning.

Now the idea of discerning by fruits came from Christ, but whence this idea of discerning by roots (that is, by the book's origins)? Just where did that come from anyway? Is it not significant that those choosing to judge the Bible by its roots have never come to faithful conclusions about its origins? Do we really want to reject the Book of Mormon with a standard that is equally, if not more, damaging to the credibility of the Bible? For example, try to find a higher critic who believes that Moses wrote the books of Moses, that Isaiah actually wrote the sixty-six chapters attributed to him, that David wrote the Psalms ascribed to him, that Solomon is the author of Proverbs, or that Matthew and John wrote the books bearing their names. If you want to quibble with scholars over this matter according to their rules of scholarship, you will lose— the Bible is not what it professes to be. But if you want to apply the test of the Savior and taste the fruits of the Bible, you will win—it is all that it professes to be and more.

We cannot all be scholars and know all that our schools have to teach, but we can all be spiritual and learn those things that the Spirit has to teach. Again we turn to Christ for a standard by which all men might know truth. His words were: "My doctrine is not mine, but his that sent me. If any man will do his will, he shall know of the doctrine, whether it be of God, or whether I speak of myself." (John 7:16–17.) Now, we can all do that; we can live a Christlike life and see if it doesn't bring a Christlike spirit. But we can't do it if we refuse to read the book or hear it read simply because it is fashionable among scholars to question its authorship.

Testing the Joseph Smith Story

The Christian faith centers in the testimonies of Matthew, Mark, Luke, and John—all devout followers of Christ. Suppose instead that the only records that had been preserved of what Christ did and taught had been written by Caiaphas, Annas, the Sanhedrin that condemned him to death, and Judas? What would people think of Jesus then? Similarly, what of those today who refuse Joseph Smith a fair hearing, having read all they need to know, as they say, from material supplied by the local Christian bookstore, material that is unfactual and deliberately misleading?

Many can testify that the suggestion that this literature does not represent truth and ought not be distributed falls on deaf ears, as does the request that they carry something that represents Mormonism fairly. Again the test applies: as Caiaphas's and Judas's are known by their fruits, so stores are known by the things they market, as are the organizations that they represent. In contrast, those who honestly seek truth will use an honest standard in the search.

Testing the Book of Abraham

The Book of Abraham provides us with the classic scriptural case study of scholarly entanglement in roots with total disregard for fruits. The lack of the autographs (original manuscripts) from which the Bible has come denies scholars the opportunity of attesting their authenticity. Theologians argue that this was deliberate on God's part to avoid our making the manuscripts an object of worship. Likewise, the Lord has not left in our possession the plates from which the Book of Mormon came. It is often argued that the latter illustrates that they never existed. We will maintain that if the world can have the Bible without the autographs, we can have the Book of Mormon without the plates, with the same reasoning that the Lord did not want anything to detract our attention from the message of the book.

That this is precisely what would happen is illustrated in the apparently endless arguments over Joseph Smith's translation of the Book of Abraham. In the instance of the Abraham papyrus, most of which is believed to have been destroyed in the great Chicago Fire of 1871, we have a few fragments that have been preserved and are in the Church's possession, along with the facsimilies published in the book (which are rough copies of what Joseph Smith translated). From what has been preserved for us, the critics of the Prophet confidently agree that his translation could not possibly be correct. However, it cannot be without significance that they cannot agree among themselves as to what the translation ought to be.

Now the question is, does the Lord expect us all to be experts in ancient languages and manuscripts so that we might authenticate the Bible and know that it is what it purports to be? Does he expect us also to be archaeologists, geologists, and metallurgists so that we might examine the gold plates and know of their verity? And does he expect us to be able to sit in judgment on the present popular and purportedly scholarly debates over the Book of Abraham? Or did he give us a test by which all men might judge whether a work is of the Lord?

Let us suggest an illustration. Suppose someone brought us a beautiful loaf of bread, hot out of the oven, delicious looking and with a marvelous aroma. Suppose also that we wanted to know whether it was good to the taste. Two possibilities suggest themselves. We could get various cooks to debate the recipe or we could just go ahead and taste it. Without demeaning the importance of cooks or scholars, Christ's suggestion is that spiritual nourishment comes from tasting, not debating.

Mormons and Their Critics

What effect does believing in the Book of Mormon have on someone? What side effects result from believing the Joseph Smith story or accepting the Book of Abraham as true? What happens to someone when they join the Mormon Church? Does it shorten their life or lengthen it? Does it make them sour and mean or does it make them pleasant and happy? We call upon their critics to respond.

Under the caption "Booklet Aims Attack at LDS," the following recently appeared in newspapers throughout the nation: "LONDON (AP)—A Roman Catholic publishing firm here says it has printed an 18-page booklet attacking the Mormon Church 'because Mormon missionaries knock on so many doors,' and it wanted to inform Catholics about the American church's beliefs.

"The booklet, entitled 'The Latter-day Saints,' says the church is a 'sect which teaches blasphemy and lies in the name of Christianity.' " Continuing, the article notes that the first page of the pamphlet states: "Most Mormons are pillars of the community, shining examples of Christian endeavor."[2]

The roots, we are told, are "blasphemy and lies," while the fruits make of its members "pillars of the community" and "shining examples of Christian endeavor." Perhaps we ought to leave well enough alone. Were we to tell a farmer that the tree that produced his prize apples had bad roots, do you think he would cut it down?

A few years ago an article appeared in *Christianity Today* entitled "Why Your Neighbor Joined the Mormon Church." Five reasons were given and are quoted here as given in the article:

1. The Mormons show genuine love and concern by taking care of the needs of their people.
2. The Mormons strive to build the family unit.
3. The Mormons provide for their young people.
4. The Mormon church is a layman's church.
5. The Mormons believe that Divine Revelation is the basis for their practices.

After briefly discussing how Mormons do the above, the article concludes: "In a day when many are hesitant to claim that God has said anything definitive, the Mormons stand out in contrast, and many people are ready to listen to what the Mormons think the voice of God says. It is tragic that their message is false, but it is nonetheless a lesson to us that people are many times ready to hear a voice of authority.

"So if your neighbor has just joined the Mormon church, I sorrow with you — particularly because I am quite sure that the appeal the church has for your neighbor was an appeal that should have come just as loud and just as clear from an evangelical church, which then could have given him the true Word of Life."[3]

Here we are being offered good roots without the fruits. Everyone must choose for himself, but "as for me and my house" we will stick with the fruits of following the path of the Savior and take fruits over roots any day.

Conclusion

So that none might be without a sure path to follow, Mormon said, "I show unto you the way to judge; for every thing which inviteth to do good, and to persuade to believe in

Christ, is sent forth by the power and gift of Christ; wherefore ye may know with a perfect knowledge it is of God. But whatsoever thing persuadeth men to do evil, and believe not in Christ, and deny him, and serve not God, then ye may know with a perfect knowledge it is of the devil; for after this manner doth the devil work, for he persuadeth no man to do good, no, not one; neither do his angels; neither do they who subject themselves unto him." (Moroni 7:16–17.) If the true purpose of all that we did were known, the source of its inspiration would also be known. All that properly represents God must pass the purity-of-purpose test.

Purity of purpose produces pure fruits. The signs, that is the fruits, always follow them that believe. "In my name," Christ said, "they shall do many wonderful works," they shall cast out devils, heal the sick, and give sight to the blind, hearing to the deaf, and speech to the dumb (see D&C 84:65–72). As Paul said of the gospel he taught, it came not in word only but "in power, and in the Holy Ghost, and in much assurance" (1 Thessalonians 1:5). "In every nation," Peter testified, "he that feareth [God], and worketh righteousness, is accepted with him" (Acts 10:35). So it has ever been and so it will ever be: "By their fruits ye shall know them" (Matthew 7:20).

CHAPTER 8

Modern Korihors
and the Art of Deception

The curriculum in Satan's schools of beguilement is timeless. The ancient crafts of deception intended to dissuade the Saints and turn aside the unwary remain little changed in our day. It is a Book of Mormon character named Korihor who provides us a classic case study.

Behold a Liberator

Our story begins toward the end of the seventeenth year of the reign of the judges, about 74 B.C. Our text is Alma 30 (we will cite it hereafter only by verse). Nestled in between the Nephite and Lamanite wars, it is one of those rare periods of peace. Our cast consists of a nation of people who sought to keep the commandments of God and were strict even in the observance of the law of Moses. Our drama begins in the land of Zarahemla; entering the scene and moving quickly to center stage is a man calling himself Korihor. He is, we are told, "Anti-Christ" (v. 12) for he denies both prophecy and the coming of Christ. He is bold, for he knows that the law will not punish a man for his beliefs and that he is free to speak them. He attracts many and is, as we shall see, both clever and articulate. We listen as he speaks:

> O ye that are bound down under a foolish and a vain hope, why do ye yoke yourselves with such foolish things? Why do ye look for a Christ? For no man can know of anything which is to come.
>
> Behold, these things which ye call prophecies, which ye say are handed down by holy prophets, behold, they are foolish traditions of your fathers.
>
> How do ye know of their surety? Behold, ye cannot know of things which ye do not see; therefore ye cannot know that there shall be a Christ.
>
> Ye look forward and say that ye see a remission of your sins. But behold, it is the effect of a frenzied mind; and this derangement of your minds comes because of the traditions of your fathers, which lead you away into a belief of things which are not so. (Vv. 13–16.)

The talk continues at length as Korihor reasons with his audience, saying much that is pleasing to the carnal mind. He emphasizes that there is no sin, for sin is but the breaking of the bands of tradition with which the people have been bound. And if there is no sin then certainly there is no need for an atonement, and if there is no atonement certainly there is no need for a Christ. Every man fared, he argued, according to "the management of the creature"; they prospered according to their genius, and conquered according to their strength—hardly a sin or crime but rather a requirement of life, he reasoned.

And so the plot unfolds. Korihor claims the protection of law in a free nation to teach the doctrines of disbelief, disrespect, and disobedience. He attempts to convince people that they are in bondage, for if he can successfully do so they will naturally turn to him as a liberator or redeemer. His then is a liberation movement. He is going to free them from the burden of commandments and gospel commitments.

Whereas the gospel declares that the knowledge of revealed truths brings freedom, Korihor contends that freedom really means being without the constraints of righteousness.

It is from their allegiance to Christ and commitment to righteousness that Korihor sought to liberate the people. He caused some of them to "lift up their heads in their wickedness," that is, to come out of the closet and take pride in those things that are an offense to God. And so we read that he led away "many women [and then almost as if it were an afterthought] and also men, to commit whoredoms—telling them that when a man was dead, that was the end thereof" (v. 18). The passage has a natural kinship with Paul's description of those in the last days who would "creep into houses, and lead captive silly women laden with sins, led away with divers lusts. . . ." And then, emphasizing that the whole thing was to be a respectable and intellectual movement, Paul described such people as "ever learning, and never able to come to the knowledge of the truth." (See 2 Timothy 3:6–7.)

The Art of Building Straw Men

Encouraged with his success among the Nephites in Zarahemla, Korihor then went among the Lamanite converts in Jershon. He found, however, that they were not as broadminded as the Nephites had been, or, as the scripture states, they were "more wise," for they bound him and took him to Ammon, their high priest. Ammon, who obviously believed in some forms of censorship, had him carried out of their land. Korihor then went to the land of Gideon, where he had considerable success until some, in protest, had him taken to the high priest and chief judge of that land.

Not only did Korihor contend boldly with the high priest, Giddonah, but he did so very cleverly. This ancient craft which he practiced so well has not been lost to modern writers of anti-Mormon literature. In the midst of his argument with Giddonah, Korihor said, "Ye say that this people is a guilty and a fallen people, because of the transgression of a parent. Behold, I say that a child is not guilty because of its parents." (V. 25.) This argument is called a straw man. That is, he attributed to Giddonah something that Giddonah does not believe—the idea that children inherit guilt through Adam's transgression. Korihor knows that he cannot fight truth fairly and come off victorious, so he attributes bad doctrine to Giddonah, a straw man to which he can give a good verbal licking.

The straw man device seems to be a mandatory ploy in attacks on the doctrines of the Church. The so-called Adam-God doctrine is a classic illustration. According to this doctrine, Latter-day Saints worship Adam as God. Now, if it were not for the anti-Mormon writings there is scarcely a soul in the Church to whom such an idea would ever have occurred. It is certainly not taught in our scriptures, and it is not found in our lesson manuals. There is not a soul in the Church that has ever heard it taught, and it is likely that nobody even knows anybody who thinks they might know someone that believes it.

It is usually necessary to prop the straw man up by quoting some Mormon leader as having made some supporting comment. The rule here is to never quote anyone still living, and the longer they have been dead the safer you are. Played with the Bible, the game can actually be a lot of fun. For instance, in the Book of Genesis we are told that Jacob made an agreement with Laban that his wages for tending Laban's herds would be the speckled and spotted cattle, sheep, and goats. Thereafter, Jacob induced the herds to give birth to speckled and spotted offspring by having them look at a striped stick when they conceived. (See Genesis 30:31–40.) Now, since Jews believe the Book of Genesis to be the word of God and hold Jacob to be a prophet, it naturally follows that all Jews believe that whatever impresses the mind of the female at the time of conception and gestation will have a corresponding influence on the mind or body of the fetus.

And, of course, since most Jews don't know they believe this, it is up to us to get the word out. The advantage of not having Jacob still with us is obvious.

Regarding Christians and the New Testament, if Paul said something they are duty bound to believe it. Thus, women are to keep silent in church (see 1 Corinthians 14:34), are not to teach (see 1 Timothy 2:12), are to keep their heads covered (see 1 Corinthians 11:5), and ought to have long hair (see 1 Corinthians 11:15). The illustrations are ridiculous, but not more so than allowing avowed enemies to tell us what we believe or than those professing to be truth seekers listening only to what our enemies have to say about us. If an honest man wanted to know what Christ taught and believed, would he seek that information from Christ or from the Sadduccees and Pharisees?

Projection, or Who's Guilty of What?

Realizing that Korihor was so given up to wickedness, and that nothing they could say would be listened to, neither Giddonah nor the chief judge attempted any response to him. Their example is one of wisdom. Rather than partake of the spirit of contention with Korihor, they had him delivered to Alma, the presiding high priest of the Church.

Korihor continued his act before Alma, reviling against the priests and teachers, "accusing them of leading away the people after the silly traditions of their fathers, for the sake of glutting on the labors of the people" (v. 31). The ploy here is what psychiatrists call projection, the unconscious act of ascribing to others one's own evil designs and desires. The Church had no paid ministry. Alma labored with his own hands for his support, never having received so much as a dime ["senine"] for his service in the Church, notwithstanding all his labors and travels in behalf of the Saints (vv. 32–35). The same was true of all the officers and teachers in the Church. Such, however, were not the desires of Korihor.

Note how well those playing Korihor's game have been described in the scripture: "Cursed are all those that shall lift up the heel against mine anointed, saith the Lord, and cry they have sinned when they have not sinned before me, saith the Lord, but have done that which was meet in mine eyes, and which I commanded them. But those who cry transgression do it because they are the servants of sin, and are the children of disobedience themselves." (D&C 121:16–17.) Those making accusations against God's anointed tell little about the Lord's servants and much about themselves. Their desires, we have learned, are very much in the image and likeness of their accusations.

The Burden of Proof

At this point Alma, himself a judge and a man who knows the rules of evidence, teaches us a great lesson in responding to the challenges of our adversaries. He asked Korihor if he believed that there was a God. Korihor responded that he did not. Alma then gave Korihor his day in court—he invited him to produce whatever evidence he could to prove the nonexistence of God (v. 40). He did not himself assume the obligation to prove to Korihor that God existed. Rather he challenged Korihor to prove that God did not. He who asserts must prove. Such is the rule of law. If I offer you money in payment of a debt and you refuse to accept it on the pretense that it is counterfeit, the burden of proof is yours. You must prove it counterfeit; it is not my obligation to prove it is genuine.

Now, we ask, have the united efforts of all the Korihors the world has ever known successfully proved that there is no God? Have they proved that Jesus was not the Christ, the promised Messiah? Where is the man that can refute the testimony of those humble shepherds who heard the heavenly host sing, and who found the infant child wrapped in swaddling clothes, lying in a manger? Who is it that can come forth and refute the testimony of the wise men who followed the star and paid homage to the Christ child? Who is it that can discredit the testimony of John that the heavens were opening to him and that he heard a voice saying, "This is my beloved son"?

Can the combined wisdom of the ages refute the reality of the resurrection? How can anyone prove that Christ did not break the bands of death? And what of the testimony of Peter who said of himself and his fellow Apostles: "We are witnesses of all things which he did both in the land of the Jews, and in Jerusalem; whom they slew and hanged on a tree: Him God raised up the third day, and shewed him openly; not to all the people, but unto witnesses chosen before of God, even to us, who did eat and drink with him after he rose from the dead." (Acts 10:39–42.)

And what of the testimony of Joseph Smith and Sidney Rigdon that the heavens were opened to them: "And now, after the many testimonies which have been given of him, this is the testimony, last of all, which we give of him: That he lives! For we saw him, even on the right hand of God; and we heard the voice bearing record that he is the Only Begotten of the Father." (D&C 76:22–23.) Who with authority can deny such a testimony? What evidence does one present to an unbiased jury to prove that on a beautiful spring morning in the year of 1820 the heavens were not opened, that the Father and the Son did not appear to the youthful Joseph Smith? How does one disprove the testimony of a prophet? "I had seen a vision," Joseph testified; "I knew it, and I knew that God knew it, and I could not deny it, neither dared I do it; at least I knew that by so doing I would offend God, and come under condemnation" (JS—H 1:25).

We accept the feelings of the Spirit or we reject them, but we do not argue them. The Sadducees and Pharisees taunted Jesus for proof, yet when it was presented in overwhelming abundance they continued to disbelieve. Be assured that when such people seek proof, that proof is the last thing in the world that they really want. As to the Korihors, we need not assume the burden of proof that is rightly theirs. If they assert we are without a God, without prophets, and without revelation, it is for them to prove it. We await that proof as have the Saints of God from the days of Adam.

Sign Seekers

Unable to accept the challenge of proof yet remaining undaunted, Korihor now demands a sign of Alma. In the meantime Alma had said to Korihor, "I know that thou believest, but thou art possessed with a lying spirit, and ye have put off the Spirit of God that it may have no place in you; but the devil has power over you, and he doth carry you about, working devices that he may destroy the children of God" (v. 42).

How interesting is Alma's insight! Alma tells us that Korihor in fact believes that which he is denying. He indicates that Korihor is little more than a wooden puppet, one dressed as a spiritual liberator, dancing and singing as his strings are pulled by the devil himself. And how appropriate that he now demand a sign, for we know that it is the "wicked and adulterous" (Matthew 16:4) that seek after signs. "The Lord said to me in a revelation," Joseph Smith reported, "that any man who wanted a sign was an adulterous person."[1]

How perfect the profile: Korihor, the anti-Christ, remitting sins in the doctrine that there is no sin, offering himself as a redeemer or liberator to a people in bondage to the errors of their fathers! Thus by accommodating the sins of others, Korihor could freely indulge in his own.

Now drunken with his own rhetoric, Korihor demands signs and the Lord accommodates him. He is struck dumb (v. 50).

Korihor now pleads with the servant of the Lord that the privilege of speech which he had so abused be returned to him. His is a written confession: "I always knew that there was a God. But behold, the devil hath deceived me; for he appeared unto me in the form of an angel, and said unto me: Go and reclaim this people, for they have all gone astray after an unknown God. And he said unto me: There is no God; yea, and he taught me that which I should say. And I have taught his words; and I taught them because they were pleasing unto the carnal mind; and I taught them, even until I had much success, insomuch that I verily believed that they were true." (Vv. 52–53.)

Despised by Those Who Flattered Them

The conclusion to our story holds no surprises, for there is a consistency in such things. To those who lift up their heel against the Lord's anointed in our day, he has said: "Those who swear falsely against my servants, that they might bring them into bondage and death—Wo unto them; because they have offended my little ones they shall be severed from the ordinances of mine house. Their basket shall not be full, their houses and their barns shall perish, and they themselves shall be despised by those that flattered them." (D&C 121: 18–20.)

Korihor pleaded with Alma to restore his speech. But Alma replied, "If this curse should be taken from thee thou wouldst again lead away the hearts of this people; therefore, it shall be unto thee even as the Lord will" (v. 55). The Lord apparently thought Korihor less harmful in silence, for his speech was not restored.

The concluding scene of our drama finds Korihor going from house to house begging food for his support. "And it came to pass that as he went forth among the people, yea, among a people who had separated themselves from the Nephites and called themselves Zoramites . . . , behold, he was run upon and trodden down, even until he was dead" (v. 59).

Conclusion

We did not borrow the Book of Mormon from the ancients; they wrote it to us. We are the audience Mormon and Moroni addressed as they chose what was to be included in this scriptural record. They told us the story of Korihor because they knew that we would have our Korihors. The Korihor of the Book of Mormon story is but the prototype of our modern anti-Christs. As the modern man of faith is in the image and likeness of his ancient counterpart, believing and testifying of those truths of which the ancients believed and testified, so the modern anti-Christ but echoes the arguments and sophistry used to beguile the souls of men anciently. Invariably, Korihors are articulate and carry with them an air of sophistication. They thrive on controversy, debate, and contention, yet inevitably their popularity rests in their appeal to the carnal nature of man.

The scriptures are remarkably explicit in profiling those given up to the lusts of the flesh. Theirs is a well-trodden path, and its effects on its travelers are easily recognized. The path is broad, for it has accommodated many sizable groups — in fact one is rarely seen traveling its shaded declines alone. Having freed themselves from the restraints of virtue and the obligations of faith, they seek to liberate us all. Temperance, humility, and godliness, in any form, they find quite unfashionable. Their preference is for banners, slogans, and a cause to protest. They have abandoned the childish lamps of testimony that may once have burned brightly. Among such the quiet assurances of the Spirit have been replaced with loudness and boisterousness, the volume of which indicates the extent of their fears.

Nephi described them as revilers against that which is good and prophesied that they would be found stirring up men to anger against the truth. They would deny revelation, he told us, profess reason, and offer little more than emotion. (See 2 Nephi 28:4–20.) Describing such, the Apostle Peter said, "the way of truth shall be evil spoken of" by them. He said they would be "presumptuous," "selfwilled," and "not afraid to speak evil of dignities." They are to be found, Peter said, speaking "evil" of things "they understand not" with "great swelling words of vanity." Their promise is one of "liberty," yet they themselves are "servants of corruption." (See 2 Peter 2.)

CHAPTER 9

A Sense of the Sacred

To every man is given a needful portion. God has entrusted to each that which is entitled to a sacred silence. Within the gospel there are truths, ordinances, and experiences "unlawful to be uttered."

The Portion of the Word

It is the will of the heavens that all men receive truth according to their ability to decipher and digest eternal verities. "God hath not revealed anything to Joseph," the Prophet declared, "but what He will make known unto the Twelve, and even the least Saint may know all things *as fast as he is able to bear them.*"[1] This concept demonstrates both divine wisdom and mercy. Men ought not to receive more than they are ready to receive; the Lord would never want to drown one in the living waters!

The Holy Ghost serves as a personal tutor. "The Comforter knoweth all things" (D&C 42:17); he knows the hearts

of all men and the readiness of individuals and congregations
to be taught the things of God. No one rushes into the presence of the Lord; likewise, no one should be ushered prematurely into the realm of divine experience. Alma responded to Zeezrom's question concerning the resurrection
by teaching a marvelous lesson:

> And now Alma began to expound these things unto him,
> saying: It is given unto many to know the mysteries of God;
> nevertheless they are laid under a strict command that they
> shall not impart only according to the portion of the word which
> he doth grant unto the children of men, according to the heed
> and diligence which they give unto him.
> And therefore, he that will harden his heart, the same re-
> ceiveth the lesser portion of the word; and he that will not
> harden his heart, to him is given the greater portion of the word,
> until it is given unto him to know the mysteries of God until
> he know them in full.
> And they that will harden their hearts, to them is given the
> lesser portion of the word until they know nothing concerning
> his mysteries; and then they are taken captive by the devil, and
> led by his will down to destruction. Now this is what is meant
> by the chains of hell. (Alma 12:9–11.)

Those charged with proclaiming the gospel message are to
be sensitive to the Spirit, discerning enough to recognize that
"portion of the word" suited to those being taught. Full-time
missionaries, for example, are given a specific commission to
teach that portion of the word necessary to introduce sincere
investigators to the message of the Restoration. They are not
commissioned to teach doctrines that could be more easily
understood and appreciated after baptism and the reception
of the Holy Ghost. Their specific assignment is to "declare
glad tidings," the tidings that the Lord has spoken anew in
our day through modern prophets, and to proclaim that the
truthfulness of the message may be tested through the Book
of Mormon. "And of tenets thou shalt not talk, but thou shalt
declare repentance and faith on the Savior, and remission of
sins by baptism, and by fire, yea, even the Holy Ghost."

(D&C 19: 29, 31.) We are to teach those outside the Church how to get into the Church, and thereafter allow the Holy Ghost to teach the fulness of the gospel. "And this is my gospel—repentance and baptism by water, and then cometh the baptism of fire and the Holy Ghost, even *the Comforter, which showeth all things, and teacheth the peaceable things of the kingdom*" (D&C 39:6; emphasis added). The Lord explained to Joseph Smith and Sidney Rigdon that "the time has verily come that it is necessary and expedient in me that *you should open your mouths in proclaiming my gospel*, the things of the kingdom, expounding the mysteries thereof out of the scriptures, *according to that portion of Spirit and power which shall be given unto you, even as I will*" (D&C 71:1; emphasis added; compare 84:85).

In the meridian of time Jesus Christ was certainly cautious as to how sacred matters were to be taught and distributed. We do not need to search the New Testament record very carefully to discover numerous occasions when the Savior instructed those closest to him to use care in speaking of things sacred. "Go ye into the world," he commanded his disciples, "saying unto all, Repent, for the kingdom of heaven has come nigh unto you. *And the mysteries of the kingdom ye shall keep within yourselves;* for it is not meet to give that which is holy unto the dogs; neither cast ye your pearls unto swine, lest they trample them under their feet. *For the world cannot receive that which ye, yourselves, are not able to bear;* wherefore ye shall not give your pearls unto them, lest they turn again and rend you." (JST, Matthew 7:9–11; emphasis added.)

One of the major reasons why Christ chose to speak in parables was to veil meaning and deeper intent from those with spiritually insensitive souls and deaf ears. "Why speakest thou unto them in parables?" the disciples asked. "He answered and said unto them, Because *it is given unto you to know the mysteries of the kingdom of heaven, but to them it is not given.*" (Matthew 13:10–11.)

The things of God are to be grasped through the Spirit of God, or they will be understood not at all (see 1 Corinthians 2:11–14). To present sacred teachings or ordinances to those lacking the gift of the Holy Ghost (and thus the lenses through which holy things may be properly seen) is to risk immediate misunderstanding and subsequent misrepresentation. *"It is not always wise,"* taught Joseph Smith, *"to relate all the truth. Even Jesus, the Son of God, had to refrain from doing so,* and had to restrain His feelings many times for the safety of Himself and His followers, and had to conceal the righteous purposes of His heart in relation to many things pertaining to His Father's kingdom."[2]

And thus it is that the Latter-day Saints are possessors and stewards over sacred matters, holy things "unlawful to be uttered." Some experiences are ineffable, so transcendently glorious that they defy human expression or description. Of these things it is not *possible* for man to utter. Joseph Smith spoke of the Father and Son as "two glorious Personages, whose brightness and glory defy all description" (JS—H 1:17). The Nephite disciples attempted to describe their experience with the resurrected Lord as he knelt and prayed unto the Father: "The eye hath never seen, neither hath the ear heard, before, so great and marvelous things as we saw and heard Jesus speak unto the Father; and no tongue can speak, neither can there be written by any man, neither can the hearts of men conceive so great and marvelous things as we both saw and heard Jesus speak; and no one can conceive of the joy which filled our souls at the time we heard him pray for us unto the Father." (3 Nephi 17:16–17; compare 19:31–34.)

Some truths and experiences are "unlawful to be uttered" in the sense that it is not *permitted* for those within the fold to share them with a doubting world; some special things are to be kept within the household of faith, among those who believe (see Moses 1:42, 4:32). The Lord explained in a revelation given in August of 1831: "Remember that *that which cometh from above is sacred, and must be spoken with care, and by constraint of the Spirit; and in this there is no condemnation"* (D&C 63:64). Members of the Church who have been endowed in the temple, for example, are under covenantal obligation to keep sacred the things taught and received therein.

Because there are ordinances and practices within the temples which are not public and thus not open for public review, enemies of the Church are eager to point out the *cultic* nature of Mormonism. If Mormons are cultic, then surely — for reasons we have already cited — Jesus of Nazareth was a cultist also, for there were matters which the Master chose to make known only to those willing and able to receive them. Elder Boyd K. Packer has written:

> Our reluctance to speak of the sacred temple ordinances is not in any way an attempt to make them seem more mysterious or to encourage an improper curiosity about them. The ordinances and ceremonies of the temple are simple. They are beautiful. They are sacred. They are kept confidential lest they be given to those who are unprepared. Curiosity is not a preparation. Deep interest itself is not a preparation. Preparation for the ordinances includes preliminary steps: faith, repentance, baptism, confirmation, worthiness, a maturity and dignity worthy of one who comes invited as a guest into the house of the Lord. . . . Some things concerning the temple ordinances have been published by apostates who seek to injure or destroy the Church. Their accounts do not assist understanding, partly because the accounts are usually distorted. In any case the temple ordinances cannot be understood without the feeling and the spiritual presence that surrounds them in the temple. They must make very dull reading indeed for the enemy who has no right to the Spirit of the Lord. [3]

Condemnation is the consequence for uttering the unutterable. President Brigham Young explained simply that "the Lord has no confidence in those who reveal secrets, for He cannot safely reveal Himself to such persons." [4] In the words of President Marion G. Romney: "*I do not tell all I know; I have never told my wife all I know, for I have found* out that *if I talked too lightly of sacred things, thereafter the Lord would not trust me.*"⁵

Milk Before Meat

The greatest man to ever walk the earth was not given access to the eternal reservior of truth before he was ready to receive it. Jesus Christ "received not the fulness [of the glory of the Father] at first, but continued from grace to grace, until [in the resurrection] he received a fulness" (D&C 93:13). Even though he possessed a fulness of the Spirit (see JST, John 3:34), he received the endowments of light and truth as he was able to bear them. Such is and should be the pattern for all those who aspire to the righteousness of the Son of God.

It is to Paul that we turn for the perfect analogy of teaching and receiving things in a certain order. He wrote to the Corinthians: "And I, brethren, could not speak unto you as unto spiritual, but as unto carnal, even as unto babes in Christ. *I have fed you with milk, and not with meat: for hitherto you were not able to bear it,* neither yet now are ye able." (1 Corinthians 3:1–2; emphasis added; see D&C 19:21–22.) Just as it would be unwise and dangerous to feed strong meat to infants, so also it is unwise and dangerous to provide deeper doctrines or sacred ordinances for public display. Too frequently those who encounter these things prematurely are unable to digest them properly, and ultimately turn with bitterness against the very source of truth.

An account of a conversation between Peter and Clement is particularly insightful in this regard. Peter instructed: "The teaching of all doctrine has a certain order: there are some things which must be delivered first, others in the second place, and others in the third, and so on, everything in its order. *If these things be delivered in their order they become plain; but if they be brought forward out of order, they will seem to be spoken against reason.*"⁶ In short, it matters a great deal not only *what* people are taught, but also *when* they are taught it. Latter-day Saints therefore have every right—and surely are under obligation in regard to their stewardship over the sacred—to treat delicately those pearls which have been given only for the people of God already initiated into the fold through the first principles and ordinances of the gospel.

Conclusion

Every man is given a needful "portion of the word." To the degree that he opens his heart to the things of God, he will be granted an additional endowment of light and truth. As he grows in understanding, however, he becomes aware of the fact that he must act with prudence in regard to disclosing sacred matters: the Spirit of the Lord is the means by which one is prompted to share the sacred; it is the means also by which the sacred may be comprehended. In a day when the Latter-day Saints are attacked on all sides for their participation in what the world perceives to be mysterious, esoteric practices, we do well to keep in mind that the Savior of mankind used judgment and care with regard to how and when he taught doctrine. He was thus extremely kind to those who were less than kind to him. So it is in our day. We will not reveal and disclose the sacred because the dull of hearing will not hear. To do so would be unchristian and unkind. Rather, we will be about our Father's business, and let the Lord confound our enemies in his own due time.

We look forward with eager anticipation to that great day when all will grow up in the Lord and receive a fulness of the Holy Ghost (D&C 109:15). In that supernal age, "they shall teach no more every man his neighbour, and every man his brother, saying, Know the Lord: for they shall all know me, from the least of them unto the greatest of them, saith the Lord" (Jeremiah 31:34). In that era those who will receive shall receive, and "the earth shall be full of the knowledge of the Lord, as the waters cover the sea" (Isaiah 11:9).

CHAPTER 10

Wisdom in Response

It is said that two things are inevitable—taxes and death; three if you are a Latter-day Saint—people asking questions about your beliefs. Most questions will be honest and sincere; others will be a sword that seeks to cut and slay. It is important that we answer honest questions well; the others are of little consequence. Yet even then we have that feeling that the gospel need not be embarrassed. No one can have all the answers, and for that matter, in many instances there may not be any one best answer. Still there are basic principles that can aid in obtaining the Spirit and in giving appropriate answers. This chapter suggests ten such principles.

Do Not Always Respond

"To every thing there is a season, and a time to every purpose under the heaven: A time to be born, and a time to die; a time to plant, and a time to pluck up that which is planted; . . . A time to rend, and a time to sew; a time to keep silence, and a time to speak." (Ecclesiastes 3:1–2, 7.) On a certain occasion the Savior charged his disciples "that they should tell no man that he was Jesus the Christ" (Matthew 16:20). The spirit of that instruction is captured in Robert Bolt's marvelous play, *A Man for All Seasons.* As the law hedges in about Sir Thomas More, this great and courageous man who will yet be a martyr for principle's sake declares: "God made the angels to show him splendor—as he made animals for innocence and plants for their simplicity. But Man he made to serve him wittily, in the tangle of his mind! If he suffers us to fall to such a case that there is no escaping, then we may stand to our tackle as best we can, and yes, . . . then we may clamor like champions . . . if we have the spittle for it. And no doubt it delights God to see splendor where He only looked for complexity. But it's God's part, not our own, to bring ourselves to that extremity! Our natural business lies in escaping."[1]

Those to whom Christ spoke were also rewarded with a martyr's death, but not one which they sought, for it sought them soon enough. Similarly we need not be spiritual martyrs bleeding with every dart and arrow shot from the bow of the adversary. In truth he is a bad shot, with a quiver full with arrows that more nearly resemble boomerangs. Let us be content to be about our business. We have greater things to do than to welcome with open arms those who would do us harm. It is for us wise counsel, as it was for the disciples of old, to "agree with thine adversary quickly, whiles thou art in the way with him" (Matthew 5:25).

Even if the question were honest and sincere we need not assume the obligation to answer it. No one has ever answered all of your questions, nor has anyone ever answered all of ours. Christ assumed no obligation to answer all questions in his day, the scriptures do not give us all the answers, and there are many questions about which we can pray that the Lord will not answer. Knowing what to pray about often requires considerable judgment. "If ye ask anything that is not expedient for you," the Lord has said, "it shall turn unto your condemnation" (D&C 88:65).

Avoid the Spirit of Contention

The gospel of Jesus Christ cannot be taught in the spirit of the adversary. The Lord said, "if ye receive not the Spirit ye shall not teach" (D&C 42:14), meaning that you cannot teach his gospel independent of his Spirit. Thus we find him telling the Nephites, "He that hath the spirit of contention is not of me, but is of the devil, who is the father of contention, and he stirreth up the hearts of men to contend with anger, one with another" (3 Nephi 11:29). Missionaries are commissioned to teach and testify, not to argue and contend. Even if the principles we teach are correct, they will be distorted if taught in the spirit of contention. The Bible teaches correct principles but not in the hands of evil and contentious people. The union of good principles and a bad spirit makes a very unpleasant marriage, which usually ends in divorce.

It is proper for us to speak against that which is untrue, even with a "loud voice" saying that it "is not of God" but "not with railing accusation" (D&C 50:32–33). If we give in to such accusation we become subject to that same spirit that we seek to oppose. We are to be articulate, bold, forthright, and honest in the defense of truth, but we are not to partake of that spirit which taunts, reviles, and berates. We do not employ Satan's legions as mercenaries to fight our battles, nor can we abandon our code of conduct, for in so doing we would give him the victory. To his own followers Satan has said: "Deceive and lie in wait to catch, that ye may destroy; behold, this is no harm." Thus we have been told "he flattereth them, and telleth them that it is no sin to lie that they may catch a man in a lie, that they may destroy him. And thus he flattereth them, and leadeth them along until he draggeth their souls down to hell; and thus he causeth them to catch themselves in their own snare." (D&C 10:25–26.) Of this spirit we want no part.

Answer the Right Question

The commission to go into all the world preaching the gospel of the kingdom is quite a different matter than a commission to go forth answering every question and responding to every objection. Countless questions can be answered to no avail. To the missionaries of our dispensation the Lord said, "Of tenets thou shalt not talk, but thou shalt declare repentance and faith on the Savior, and remission of sins by baptism, and by fire, yea, even the Holy Ghost" (D&C 19:31). By tenets the Lord means the myriad of peripheral issues that divert our attention from the principles upon which salvation rests. To have given the best of answers to the wrong questions is a bit like waking up to discover that you are married to Leah instead of Rachel.

The great question demanding an answer is, Do we have something that the world doesn't? If we don't, then why all the fuss? Let's call the missionaries home and tell the world that we are like everyone else so they can quit being offended with us. But if we have been commissioned to build anew the temple of gospel understanding, then we ought not to spend our time running around putting out theological brush fires.

The Lord doesn't expect us to marshal Bible arguments to prove that Christ is Jehovah, that we should worship on Sunday rather than Saturday, that salvation requires more than just grace, and a thousand similar issues. The Bible does not give clear answers on some of these things. Our answers have come by revelation through living prophets—that is our message to the world. The great question is, does God still speak? And we are the only people on the face of the earth with a sure answer to the question. Latter-day Saints have fought many a valiant fight on the wrong battlefield. Our message concerns living prophets, the restoration of all truths, and answers that have been revealed anew; our commission is to get that testimony into the hearts of people. We are to get them to read the Book of Mormon with a prayerful spirit. We are to testify to our friends and neighbors of Joseph Smith, and then when they have that testimony we can show them the revelations of the Restoration wherein the Lord has given the answers to their questions. Is it not more meaningful to let the Lord answer their questions than for us to do so?

Answer from the Right Source

There is no better way to let the spirit of the Restoration evidence itself than to answer those who ask questions with the revelations of the Restoration, primarily the Book of Mormon and the Doctrine and Covenants. Such a statement is virtually always met with the objection that "they don't believe those sources. Shouldn't we use the Bible because it is our common ground?" The answer is an emphatic no! First, the Bible is not common ground, it's fighting ground. The religious world has been fighting over the meaning of the Bible for thousands of years. The Bible has been the excuse for war, bloodshed, and all manner of turmoil. But the Lord added the Book of Mormon to the Bible for the purpose of "the confounding of false doctrines and laying down of contentions, and establishing peace" (2 Nephi 3:12). Questions that can be answered from the Book of Mormon should never be answered from the Bible.

Now the doubter will say, "If we answer from the Book of Mormon, we are just going to be told that it is our scripture and they don't believe it." To which we respond, "This is precisely what should happen. Now we have identified the real issue. Do we have scripture and prophets that they do not? And if they are honest, hadn't they better learn about it?" This is one of the most important lessons that we learn from Joseph Smith's experiences. As Joseph struggled to find truth, he attended meetings, listened to ministers, and asked questions about the Bible. And finally he learned that he had to ask of God for himself. For, as he said, the "teachers of religion of the different sects understood the same passages of scripture so differently as to destroy all confidence in settling the question by an appeal to the Bible" (JS—H 1:12). Bible answers can be argued, while the testimony of the Book of Mormon must be accepted or rejected. It is for the Spirit to confirm, not to contend.

Avoid the Phony Testimony Dodge

The importance of teaching by testimony cannot be over-emphasized, yet the nature of true testimony is sometimes misunderstood. Some have supposed that they can hide their lack of knowledge behind what they falsely call testimony. Where there is no knowledge there is no testimony. If we have not taught anything, we do not have anything to testify of. A testimony is a seal placed upon that which we have taught. Our competence as a witness in a court of law is predicated on knowledge, and so it is in the realm of spiritual things. We can bear competent witness only to that which we know by the Spirit of revelation. To do otherwise is to bear false witness.

None have taught these principles more perfectly than President Joseph F. Smith:

> The sanctity of a true testimony should inspire a thoughtful care as to its use. That testimony is not to be forced upon everybody, nor is it to be proclaimed at large from the housetop. It is not to be voiced merely to 'fill up the time' in a public meeting; far less to excuse or disguise the speaker's poverty of thought or ignorance of the truth he is called to expound.
>
>   . . . The over-zealous missionary may be influenced by the misleading thought that the bearing of his testimony to those who have not before heard the gospel message, is to convince or condemn, as the hearers accept or reject. The elder is sent

into the field to preach the gospel—the good news of its restoration to earth, showing by scriptural evidence the harmony of the new message with the predictions of earlier times; expounding the truths embodied in the first principles of the gospel; then if he bears his testimony under divine inspiration, such a testimony is as a seal attesting the genuineness of the truths he has declared, and so appealing to the receptive soul whose ears have been saluted by the heaven-sent message.

But the voicing of one's testimony, however eloquently phrased or beautifully expressed, is no fit or acceptable substitute for the needed discourse of instruction and counsel expected in a general gathering of the people. The man who professes a testimony as herein described, and who assumes that his testimony embraces all the knowledge he needs, and who therefore lives in indolence and ignorance shall surely discover his error to his own cost and loss. . . .

. . . Of those who speak in his name, the Lord requires humility, not ignorance. [2]

Avoid the Burden of Proof

We return now to the great lesson taught to us by Alma in his confrontation with Korihor. The rule of law, as we have learned, is that he who asserts must prove. Those whose lives have been devoid of spiritual experiences have been quick to deny to others that which they have not experienced themselves. "Does it remain," Joseph Smith asked, "for a people who never had faith enough to call down one scrap of revelation from heaven, and for all they have now are indebted to the faith of another people who lived hundreds and thousands of years before them, does it remain for them to say how much God has spoken and how much he has not spoken?"[3] For someone to argue that we have not had spiritual experiences because he hasn't is like arguing that we cannot feel good because he doesn't. If he wants to try to prove that we don't feel good, he may certainly try. It doesn't change our mood, but we hardly need to assume the obligation to prove that we do indeed feel good.

The Sadducees and Pharisees taunted Jesus for proof, and yet when it was presented in overwhelming abundance they continued to disbelieve it. Be assured that when someone seeks proof that proof is the last thing in the world that they really want. When Christ gave sight to the man born blind, the council of the Jews found no reason to rejoice in his good fortune; rather, they were greatly angered. Again and again they cross-examined him in the search for some way to discount the event. Finally the jubilant man, who could now see and to whom the blindness of the Sanhedrin was becoming increasingly apparent, said, "I have told you already, and ye did not hear: wherefore would ye hear it again? will ye also be his disciples? Then they reviled him, and said, Thou art his disciple; but we are Moses' disciples. We know that God spake unto Moses: as for this fellow, we know not from whence he is. The man answered and said unto them, Why herein is a marvellous thing, that ye know not from whence he is, and yet he hath opened mine eyes." (John 9:27–30.) "I am the light which shineth in darkness," Christ testified, "and the darkness comprehendeth it not" (D&C 6:21).

Assume the Burden of Proof

It is our intent to go among every nation, kindred, tongue, and people testifying that Joseph Smith is a prophet and that the Church organized by Christ in the meridian of time has been restored anew. As we assert this, the burden of proof becomes ours, a burden we anxiously accept. We have our evidence, real and tangible, and we invite the world to examine it. It is a book like no other book on the face of the earth, a book received at the hands of an angel, a book coming forth in fulfillment of ancient prophecy, a book detailing events of the last days. It is a book with greater power to bring a person to God than any other book ever written. We speak, of course, of the Book of Mormon. Moroni, its editor and compiler, said it was written for "the convincing of the Jew and Gentile that Jesus is the Christ'' (Preface to the Book of Mormon). This book was preserved to come forth in the last days, "proving to the world that the holy scriptures are true, and that God does inspire men and call them to his holy work in this age and generation, as well as in generations of old; thereby showing that he is the same God yesterday, today, and forever'' (D&C 20:11–12).

We have been told too often that spiritual things cannot be proven, but indeed they can. "Prove me now herewith," the Lord said to those who would pay tithes and offerings, "if I will not open you the windows of heaven, and pour you out a blessing, that there shall not be room enough to receive it'' (Malachi 3:10). "Prove all things," said Paul; "hold fast that which is good" (1 Thessalonians 5:21). So we invite all to prove or test the Book of Mormon, asking page by page in their reading, "Could Joseph Smith have written this?" The book itself extends the promise that those who read it with a sincere heart and real intent will know of its truthfulness by the power of the Holy Ghost (see Moroni 10:3–5). Millions have now put the book to the test and avow the promise was fulfilled.

Answer the Question They Should Have Asked

Perhaps the most effective way to handle antagonistic, improper, or irrelevant questions is to use them as a springboard for answering the questions that should have been asked. Even if the questioner objects, you may have been able to plant good seeds in the mind of any listener who is honestly seeking the truth. Effective teachers learn to mold poor or irrelevant student questions into teaching moments that are valuable to the entire class. Similarly an experienced Church leader counseled his sons that when they are called on to speak and the person extending the invitation does not ask them to talk on what they ought to, they should have the sense to do it anyway.

Ask the Right Questions

Elder Neal A. Maxwell has made the observation that frequently we as teachers give excellent answers to questions that no one is asking. As our answers must be relevant, so must our questions.

An associate tells the story of driving across the state of Washington when he was passed by a psychedelically decorated van with a sign painted on the side that read, Former Mormons Who Have Been Saved. Now, it didn't take the spirit of discernment to tell that the long-haired and rather unkempt-looking occupants of the van were looking for confrontation with members of the Church. Sometime later he passed the van parked at an eating establishment and felt the urge to go in. The group was easily recognized and so he went over to their table and asked if they were the former Mormons who had been saved. They vocally and proudly announced themselves to be the same. He then said, "I just have one question I wanted to ask—Which commandment was it that you didn't want to keep?" The question was greeted with a strained and awkward silence.

The question cut through their well-rehearsed arguments and the faults that they had found with the Church, which served no purpose other than to justify their own failure to keep the commandments and unwillingness to honestly repent of their sins. It was much easier to prove the Church false and get saved by grace. The story is unfortunately representative of many. Far too often home teachers or others laboring with inactive members of the Church wear themselves out responding to all manner of objections to the Church, only to discover that their answers have not moved the inactive member any closer to the doors of the Church. What is needed is not answers to objections, for they would melt with the morning dew if some broken commandment could be mended. The real answer is found in extending the arm of love to those being taught. It is found in helping them develop the desire and courage to fight the lion of transgression that stands in their path. Once the lion is chased off, they can safely return to activity.

Make Your Stand at the Wall of Faith

Peter told us that we should be "ready always to give an answer to every man that asketh you a reason of the hope that is in you with meekness and fear" (1 Peter 3:15). As we ought to be articulate in answers, we must also be articulate in faith. President Ezra Taft Benson observed "that sooner or later we are all backed up against the wall of faith where we must make our stand."[4] All men of wisdom frequently have the opportunity to say, "I do not know." Men of faith will also frequently have the opportunity to say, "But this much I do know," and ignoring those things they do not understand will bear witness of those things that we cannot misunderstand.

Conclusion

Not all questions are equally deserving of an answer, nor are all who ask the questions. Christ, a tireless teacher of the gospel, would not dignify Herod's questions with a response. In contrast, he promises those who serve him in righteousness and in truth that he will reveal to them all the mysteries of his kingdom "from days of old, and for ages to come" (see D&C 76:5–10). Following those same principles we have been instructed to continually study the gospel and live worthy of the promptings of the Spirit so that we might be prepared to give that portion that should be "meted unto every man" (D&C 84:85).

CHAPTER 11

A House of Faith

In December 1832 the Lord commanded the Saints to "establish a house, even a house of prayer, a house of fasting, a house of faith, a house of learning, a house of glory, a house of order, a house of God" (D&C 88:119). Such are the building materials out of which every man ought to build his own household of faith. The House of the Lord is the pattern. Like the temple, each Latter-day Saint home ought to be a house of prayer, of fasting, of faith, of learning, of glory, of order, a house of God—that it too might be a defense and a refuge from the world.

Entering the Rest of the Lord

To have built with the proper materials is to have the confidence that one may weather every storm. Such is the house of faith, a place where one finds rest in the Lord. President Joseph F. Smith, who knew as well as any man on earth the cold and biting winds of sectarian hatred, described the rest of the Lord as "the spiritual rest and peace which are born from a settled conviction of the truth in the minds of men." This is a rest found only in an understanding of the truths of the gospel, and the "peace of the Spirit" which testifies of their divine origin.[1] President Smith further explained that entering the rest of the Lord

> means *entering into the knowledge and love of God, having faith in his purpose and in his plan, to such an extent that we know that we are right,* and that we are not hunting for something else, we are not disturbed by every wind of doctrine, or by the cunning and craftiness of men who lie in wait to deceive. *We know of the doctrine that it is of God, and we do not ask any questions* of anybody about it; they are welcome to their opinions, to their ideas and to their vagaries. The man who has reached that degree of faith in God that all doubt and fear have been cast from him, he has entered into "God's rest," and he need not fear the vagaries of men, nor their cunning and craftiness, by which they seek to deceive and mislead him from the truth. I pray that we may all enter into God's rest—rest from doubt, from fear, from apprehension of danger, rest from the religious turmoil of the world.[2]

Without question, one of the sweetest by-products of a witness of the work in which we are engaged is the peace that comes in the times of difficulty; that peace is the confirmation of the Lord that we have every reason to be secure in what we teach and believe. It is the Lord whispering: "Be still and know that I am God" (D&C 101:16). Peace is of God; what greater witness can a person have than from God? (See D&C 6:22–23.)

Laying the Foundation

Our house of faith can be no more secure than the foundation upon which it is built. Foolish men build upon the shifting sands of ethics and the marshlands of man-made philosophies and doctrines. Wise men build upon the rock of revelation, heeding carefully the living oracles, lest they be "brought under condemnation . . . , and stumble and fall when the storms descend, and the winds blow, and the rains descend, and beat upon their house" (D&C 90:5). Nephi warned the "humble followers of Christ"—zealous and well-meaning members of the Church—that they too may be misled if they do not know well the foundation upon which they must build. Of those living in the last days he said: "They have all gone astray save it be a few, who are the humble followers of Christ; nevertheless, they are led, that in many instances they do err because they are taught by the precepts of men" (2 Nephi 28:14).

The vitality of Mormonism is in its doctrines. To teach this principle, Elder Bruce R. McConkie used the following parable:

> Hear now the parable of the unwise builder. A certain man inherited a choice piece of ground whereon to build an house to shelter his loved ones from the storms of the day and the cold of the night. He began his work with zeal and skill using good materials for the need was urgent. But in his haste and because he gave no heed to the principles of proper construction, he laid no foundation; but commencing immediately, he built the floor and raised the walls and began to cover them with a roof. Then to his sorrow, because his house had no foundation, it fell and became a heap of rubble and those whom he loved had no shelter. Verily, verily, I say unto you, A wise builder, when he buildeth an house, first layeth the foundation and then buildeth thereon.
>
> Hear now the interpretation of the parable of the unwise builder. A certain church officer was called to build a house of faith and righteousness and salvation for the souls entrusted to his care. Knowing he had been called by inspiration and having great zeal, he hastened to strengthen and build up the programs of the Church without first laying the foundation of faith and testimony and conversion. He spent his time on mechanics, and means, and programs, and procedures, and leadership training; and never laid the great and eternal foundation upon which all things must rest in the Lord's house—the foundation of our theology and of our doctrine.[3]

All that we do as members of the Lord's Church must be built upon a foundation of faith and testimony and conversion. When external supports fail us, then our hearts must be riveted upon the things of the Spirit, those internal realities which provide the meaning and perspective for all else that matters.

Founded on the Eternal

To be secure the household of faith must rest upon principles that are absolute and eternal. "For do we not read that God is the same yesterday, today, and forever, and in him there is no variableness neither shadow of changing?" (Mormon 9:9.) We were schooled in the plan of salvation eons before our birth into mortality. All gospel laws were ordained and taught "before the world was" (D&C 132:11). To restore gospel knowledge is in large measure to restore past memory. True it is that priesthood and keys must be given anew from heaven, as must the ordinances and principles, but the doctrines come to the pure mind not as something new but rather as a distant memory from the past. What we have chosen to call conversion is better described as an awakening, a reminding, a remembering of truths known once long ago. It is to spiritually come home. The Apostle Paul described the gospel he taught as one that his hearers had "heard before" (Colossians 1:5), and as containing promises given "before the world began" (Titus 1:2). President Joseph F. Smith spoke of the conversion process as "the awakening of the memories of the spirit."[4] All men may gain a renewed testimony. The clarity of that distant memory from the past can be obscured by clouds of impurity or by having our hearts set too much on the things of the world, yet its imprint is etched on the soul of every man.

C. S. Lewis captured the significance of that knowledge that is born within us. He reasoned:

The convert accepted forgiveness of sins. But of sins against what Law? Some new law promulgated by the Christians? But that is nonsensical. It would be the mockery of a tyrant to forgive a man for doing what had never been forbidden until the very moment at which the forgiveness was announced. The idea (at least in its grossest and most popular form) that Christianity brought a new ethical code into the world is a grave error. If it had done so, then we should have to conclude that all who first preached it wholly misunderstood their own message: for all of them, its Founder, His precursor, His apostles, came demanding repentance and offering forgiveness, a demand and an offer both meaningless except on the assumption of a moral law already known and already broken.[5]

The point missed by Lewis is that this is equally true of all men independent of what their society or culture has taught them. All are equally obligated to accept Christ and live the gospel. The announcement that those rejecting the gospel will be damned is universal. It finds fairness only in the fact that all were taught that gospel before they were born and covenanted then to accept it.

Lewis also astutely observed that "a Christian who understands his own religion laughs when unbelievers expect to trouble him by the assertion that Jesus uttered no command which had not been anticipated by the Rabbis—few, indeed, which cannot be paralleled in classical, ancient Egyptian, Ninevite, Babylonian, or Chinese texts. We have long recognized that truth with rejoicing. Our faith is not pinned on a crank."[6] Many would argue that Joseph Smith could hardly be a prophet because others had already thought or said much of what he restored to the Saints. If valid, this argument would also dismiss any possibility that Jesus is the Christ. But it is common knowledge to Latter-day Saints that the fulness of the gospel of Jesus Christ was first had by Adam. We anticipate finding fragments of it among every kindred, tongue, and people. Again we see that the arguments used against the Church are often better suited to defend it.

Raising the Pillars

Just as the things in the natural environment may be known through the five senses, even so may the things of the spiritual realm be discerned and known by the spirit of man. A *testimony* is the internal evidence of divine communication, a revelation by the power of the Holy Ghost that a doctrine or principle or specific matter is of God and thus true. A testimony is neither mythical or imagined; it is real! In the words of Alma: "O then, is not this real? I say unto you, Yea, because it is light; and whatsoever is light, is good, because it is discernible." (Alma 32:35.) There are many things of which a member of the Church may have a testimony, but three declarative and emphatic statements are the pillars of faith in these latter days.

Jesus is the Christ. Paul taught the Corinthians that "no man can [know] that Jesus is the Lord, but by the Holy Ghost" (1 Corinthians 12:3; see also *Teachings of the Prophet Joseph Smith*, p. 223). Indeed, by the Holy Ghost all men are entitled, even obligated, to know that Jesus is the Christ. To know that Jesus is the Christ is to know that he is the promised Messiah, the hope and fulfillment of the ages; that salvation is in him; and that there is no other name given by the Father through which salvation may come to the children of men. To know that Jesus is the Christ is to know by revelation that God is literally his Father, and that from the Man of Holiness the Son inherited the powers of immortality, the right to live forever. "For as the Father hath life in himself; so hath he given to the Son to have life in himself" (John 5:26). To know that Jesus is the Christ is to know also that he inherited from Mary—his mother, a mortal woman—the powers of mortality, the right to know and experience the pulls and pressures of this fallen sphere, and eventually to encounter the universal commonality—physical death. "Therefore doth my Father love me," Jesus taught in time's meridian, "because I lay down my life, that I might take it again. No man taketh it from me, but I lay it down of myself. I have power to lay it down, and I have power to take it again." (John 10:17–18.) Lehi taught his son Jacob that "there is no flesh that can dwell in the presence of God, save it be through the merits, and mercy, and grace of the Holy Messiah, who layeth down his life according to the flesh, and taketh it again by the power of the Spirit, that he may bring to pass the resurrection of the dead, being the first that should rise" (2 Nephi 2:8).

To know that Jesus is the Christ is to know that Jesus of Nazareth did for us that which no other man could have done; it is to have the unequivocal and unshaken faith that truly "There was no other good enough / To pay the price of sin. / He only could unlock the gate / Of heaven and let us in."[7] It is to know that by means of his sinless state and his godly powers he was able to make the awful and incomprehensible atonement, and thus to bring "life and immortality to light through the gospel" (2 Timothy 1:10).

Joseph Smith is a prophet of God. Joseph Smith is a prophet of God in the sense that he is a *revealer of truth* in these latter days. "This generation," the Lord said in 1829, "shall have my word through you" (D&C 5:10). The nature and being of God the Father, the atoning mission of Jesus the Christ, and the myriad of truths and doctrines of salvation are to be learned through the teachings of Joseph Smith.

To know that Joseph Smith is a prophet of God is also to recognize him as a *legal administrator,* the means by which keys and powers and priesthoods were delivered to earth again. Because of the Prophet's instrumentality, the Church of Jesus Christ was organized; temples were built and ordinance workers were given divine authorization to bind and seal; and the ordinances of salvation were made available to the followers of righteousness. To know that Joseph Smith is a prophet is to know, as President Brigham Young boldly declared, that "no man or woman in this dispensation will ever enter into the celestial kingdom of God without the consent of Joseph Smith. From the day that the Priesthood was taken from the earth to the winding-up scene of all things, every man and woman must have the certificate of Joseph Smith, junior, as a passport to their entrance into the mansion where God and Christ are.''[8] In the final analysis, to know that Joseph Smith is a prophet of God is to know that ''Joseph Smith, the Prophet and Seer of the Lord, has done more, save Jesus only, for the salvation of men in this world, than any other man that ever lived in it'' (D&C 135:3).

The Church is divinely led today. As we noted in an earlier chapter, the Lord designated the Church as the only *true* and *living* church upon the face of the whole earth (see D&C 1:30). The true Church teaches true principles, administers true ordinances through true priesthood authority, and thus provides the only true means to salvation. To know that The Church of Jesus Christ of Latter-day Saints is the only true and living church is to acknowledge that the successors of Joseph Smith in the Presidency of the Church possess the keys and powers necessary to guide the Church in the manner prescribed by the heavens. It is to know that the Church is a vital and necessary ingredient in the cause of truth, and is now in the line of its duty. Finally, to know that the Church is divinely led is to know that the Lord is in our midst. ''There has come to me,'' President Harold B. Lee said at the conclusion of the October 1972 general conference, ''in these last few days a deepening and reassuring faith. I can't leave this conference without saying to you that I have a conviction that the Master hasn't been absent from us on these occasions. This is his church. Where else would he rather be than right here at the headquarters of his church? He isn't an absentee master; he is concerned about us. He wants us to follow where he leads. I know that he is a living reality, as is our Heavenly Father. I know it.''[9] President Joseph Fielding Smith testified: ''I desire to say that no man of himself can lead this church. It is the Church of the Lord Jesus Christ; he is at the head. The Church bears his name, has his priesthood, administers his gospel, preaches his doctrine, and does his work. . . . If this were the work of man, it would fail, but it is the work of the Lord, and he does not fail.''[10]

These three pillars are fundamental to a living witness of the truth; they are essential if one is to stand in the midst of constant assault upon the foundations of Mormonism. One may possess strong feelings about many things—the Word of Wisdom, single adult programs, youth activities, family focus, and so forth. But these three pillars of the faith provide the anchors to the soul as well as the building blocks for numerous other phases of the work.

In the period following the death and ascension of the Savior, the leaders of the Church in the first century went to all parts of the known world bearing testimony to the things they knew to be true. The physical evidence of the divine sonship of Christ in that day was the resurrection; because Jesus rose from the dead with a tangible body of flesh and bones—as he had promised—the Apostles and those to whom their witness spread could know that Jesus was indeed the Christ. In our day the Lord has likewise provided a tangible witness of the divinity of this great latter-day work: by means of the Book of Mormon, men and women the world over can gain a testimony of the truth and can raise the three pillars in constructing their own houses of faith. Any man can stand thereafter in the midst of intellectual and spiritual turmoil and can withstand the buffetings of those bent on overthrowing the kingdom of God.

To Whom the Door Is Open

The door of the household of faith is always open to that which pleases the eye, strengthens the body, gladdens the heart, and enlivens the soul (see D&C 59:18–19). Welcome guests include "whatsoever things are honest, whatsoever things are just, whatsoever things are pure, whatsoever things are lovely, whatsoever things are of good report." All that is virtuous and praiseworthy is also eagerly received. (See Philippians 4:8.) Here the honest truth seeker is always at home. Silver and gold have we but little, but such as we have we freely share.

There are those, however, to whom the door of the household of faith is not thrust open. We seek to heed the Savior's instruction to the Twelve to "beware of the leaven of the Pharisees and of the Sadducees," meaning their doctrines and hypocrisy. (See Matthew 16:6, 12; Luke 12:1.) There are those persons who seek to trample the sacred, those who, in the words of Elder Boyd K. Packer, "wade the muddy paths of opposition and apostasy. Then without changing their boots, they seek to push open the doors of the temple and stride into those hallowed precincts."[11] It may prove impossible in this age to avoid totally such influences, but, on the other hand, they need not be welcomed or sought out. They do little to strengthen the house of faith; they do much to sow seeds of darkness and doubt and discord. The Spirit of the Lord is positive, and the wise builder does all in his power to associate himself with those things which edify and enrich. It is easy to discern the source of that which maligns and defames.

The wise builder of the house of faith is likewise cautious of those who have professed to know the name of the Lord, and yet have not known him. In the words of a modern revelation, these are they who "have blasphemed against me in the midst of my house, saith the Lord" (D&C 112:26). Among such persons are those who would enter our home under the pretense of academic honesty or curiosity, but who thereafter prove to be traitors to the cause of the Restoration through evil speaking of the Lord's anointed or questioning the historicity of foundational events of this dispensation.

A more subtle but perhaps equally subversive and divisive intruder to the house of faith is that member of the Church who feels the need to place qualifiers around his commitment to the faith. Such a person—having read by the lamp of his own conceit—judges all things by the standards of the world, including many of the doctrines and practices of the Church. Elder Packer warned Church educators against proposals or projects which begin with an attitude like, " 'We are all active and faithful members of the Church; *however, . . .*' " In speaking of one such group of Latter-day Saints, Elder Packer explained: "That *however* meant that they put a condition upon their Church membership and their faith. It meant that they put something else first. It meant that they were to judge the Church and gospel and the leaders of it against their own backgrounds and training. It meant that their commitment was partial, and that partial commitment is not enough to qualify one for full spiritual light."[12] Those that say they know the Church is true and that they sustain the living prophet, "however," are following quite a different path than those who say, "We know the Church is true and we sustain the living prophet, therefore. . . ." The Lord has his own standard of judgment: "Behold, I, the Lord, have made my church in these last days like unto a judge sitting on a hill, or in a high place, to judge the nations. For it shall come to pass that the inhabitants of Zion shall judge all things pertaining to Zion." (D&C 64:37–38.)

Conclusion

The gates of hell cannot prevail against one who is secure in that knowledge which saves. "The work of righteousness," Isaiah testified anciently, "shall be peace; and the effect of righteousness quietness and assurance forever" (Isaiah 32:17; compare D&C 59:23). To be grounded in the faith and built upon the foundation of doctrine and testimony is to have entered into the rest of the Lord, a rest known only to those who have the quiet but powerful assurance that the Lord is in our midst. Latter-day Saints who have the needed witness are able to stand firm in the face of all odds and all opposition. President Gordon B. Hinckley demonstrated this through a touching story some years ago which points up the possible cost of one's membership, but also the power of one's assurance:

> Mine has been the opportunity to meet many wonderful men and women in various parts of the world. A few of them have left an indelible impression upon me. One such was a naval officer from Asia, a brilliant young man who had been brought to the United States for advanced training. Some of his associates in the United States Navy, whose behavior had attracted him, shared with him at his request their religious beliefs. He was not a Christian, but he was interested. They told him of the Savior of the world, of Jesus born in Bethlehem, who gave his life for all mankind. They told him of the appearance of God, the Eternal Father, and the resurrected Lord to the boy Joseph Smith. They spoke of modern prophets. They taught him the gospel of the Master. The Spirit touched his heart, and he was baptized.
>
> He was introduced to me just before he was to return to his native land. We spoke of these things, and then I said, "Your people are not Christians. You come from a land where Christians have had a difficult time. What will happen when you return home a Christian and, more particularly, a Mormon Christian?"
>
> His face clouded, and he replied, "My family will be disappointed. I suppose they will cast me out. They will regard me as dead. As for my future and my career, I assume that all opportunity will be foreclosed against me."
>
> I asked, "Are you willing to pay so great a price for the gospel?"
>
> His dark eyes, moistened by tears, shone from his handsome brown face as he answered, "It's true, isn't it?"
>
> Ashamed at having asked the question, I responded, "Yes, it's true."
>
> To which he replied. "Then what else matters?"
>
> These are the questions I should like to leave with you this morning: "It's true, isn't it? Then what else matters?"[13]

Such is the peace and power of testimony. Such is the substance of that which those who seek to destroy us can never destroy.

CHAPTER 12

No Weapon That Is Formed

Joseph Smith's struggle with the arch-deceiver in the Sacred Grove in the spring of 1820 was a harrowing personal encounter; it was also a type and a shadow of the evil which would engage the Kingdom of God in a battle of enormous proportions in the final dispensation. In our day designing individuals strike at the heart and core of Mormonism—they attack the very foundations of the faith of the Latter-day Saints.

Such doings, however, were known and foreknown through the ages. Note, for example, the prophetic word of David the Psalmist: "In that day thou shalt come, O Lord; and I will put my trust in thee. Thou shalt say unto thy people, for mine ear hath heard the voice; thou shalt say unto every soul, Flee unto my mountain; and the righteous shall flee like a bird that is let go from the snare of the fowler. For *the wicked bend their bow; lo, they make ready their arrow upon the string, that they may privily shoot at the upright in heart, to destroy their foundation.*" Note also the consolation given by the Lord to his people: "But the foundations of the wicked shall be destroyed, and what can they do?" (JST, Psalm 11:1–3; emphasis added.)

By Way of Summary

We have sought to state in plainness and simplicity some valuable principles of truth, the analysis of which serves in a very real way as the most eloquent defense of the faith. Members of the Lord's Church who are grounded in these principles, as well as settled and established in the doctrines and theology of the Restoration, are able to view slanderous attacks and misrepresentations with a divine perspective; most important, they are able to rest secure in the quiet but definite assurance that despite the powers of earth and hell—and the buffetings of men and demons—the Kingdom of God will come off triumphant.

In the preceding chapters we have set forth a number of important principles, perhaps the most vital of which are the following:

1. Truth is identified by the witness of the Spirit and also the opposition of the adversary.

2. To accept the prophets whom the Lord sends in one's own day is to accept the Lord who sends them.

3. Those who focus too heavily on what was *once* said (to the exclusion of what is *now being said* by those in authority) may trade plainness for blindness. To despise the living word is to despise that Lord from whence it came.

4. The Saints should beware of those who demean the Spirit by confining it to a text or a book, saying "We have enough," for from these shall be taken even that which they have. Such have a form of godliness but deny the power thereof.

5. The Lord has said that he would "call upon the weak things of the world, those who are unlearned and despised, to thrash the nations by the power of [his] Spirit" (D&C 35:13).

6. The living Church is characterized by development, change, and line-upon-line growth. Like a seed or a child growing to maturity, the Church changes in appearance without changing its identity.

7. We cannot all be scholars and know all that our schools have to teach, but we can all be spiritual and learn those things that the Spirit has to teach.

8. Far too often those who seek to "liberate" the Saints from their religious beliefs and obligations seek to remit sins with the doctrine that there is no sin; and such persons desire to proselyte the people of God to share their guilt.

9. We do not tell all we know. Christ did not tell all he knew or experienced. There is a doctrine of sacred silence. Pearls are not to be cast before swine.

10. The Saints are under no obligation to respond to all questions. An obligation is, however, laid upon them—an obligation of faith in the restored gospel—to declare with boldness those things which have been revealed through Joseph Smith the Prophet (see D&C 31:4).

11. The confidence and peaceful assurance associated with the witness of the work in which we are engaged is an anchor to the troubled soul, the means by which one is permitted to enter the quiet rest of the Lord.

By Way of Testimony

All that remains for us as authors is to bear witness of the things about which we have been speaking. Ours is the testimony that there is a God in heaven who is infinite and eternal, and in whose image man is created—the Father of our spirits; that Jesus Christ is Lord of all, the living Son of the living God, and the Author of eternal salvation; that Joseph Smith was called of God as both a legal administrator and a revealer of the nature of God to man, and that if the truths of salvation are to be had in this day, they will be delivered by and through Joseph Smith and his successors and none else; and that The Church of Jesus Christ of Latter-day Saints is the Kingdom of God on earth, is in the line of its duty, and will grow and expand until its members are found in every nation on earth. These things we know.

The Lord explained to his servant Joseph in 1831: "Verily, thus saith the Lord unto you—*there is no weapon that is formed against you shall prosper; And if any man lift his voice against you he shall be confounded in mine own due time. Wherefore, keep my commandments; they are true and faithful.*" (D&C 71:9–11; emphasis added.) The little stone cut out of the mountain without hands is rolling with accelerated force: the kingdom of God is going forth, all in preparation for that glorious kingdom of heaven yet to come (see D&C 65:2, 6). Like Peter of old, our gaze must not be affected by the winds and waves of adversity; our focus must ever be upon the Lord and his anointed servants. "For by doing these things," the Master assured the early Latter-day Saints, "*the gates of hell shall not prevail against you; yea, and the Lord God will disperse the powers of darkness from before you,* and cause the heavens to shake for your good, and his name's glory" (D&C 21:6). In the words of a modern Apostle:

> The Church is like a great caravan—organized, prepared, following an appointed course, with its captains of tens and captains of hundreds all in place.
>
> What does it matter if a few barking dogs snap at the heels of the weary travellers? Or that predators claim those few who fall by the way? The caravan moves on.
>
> Is there a ravine to cross, a miry mud hole to pull through, a steep grade to climb? So be it. The oxen are strong and the teamsters wise. The caravan moves on.
>
> Are there storms that rage along the way, floods that wash away the bridges, deserts to cross, and rivers to ford? Such is life in this fallen sphere. The caravan moves on.
>
> Ahead is the celestial city, the eternal Zion of our God, where all who maintain their position in the caravan shall find food and drink and rest. Thank God that the caravan moves on![1]

Notes

Preface

1. See Joseph Smith, *History of the Church*, 2nd ed. rev., edited by B. H. Roberts, 7 vols. (Salt Lake City: The Church of Jesus Christ of Latter-day Saints, 1932–51), 1:88–95.

2. *History of the Church*, 1:95; emphasis added.

3. *History of the Church*, 1:92.

4. *History of the Church*, 1:94.

Chapter 1. Strength in Opposition

1. James R. Clark, comp., *Messages of the First Presidency of The Church of Jesus Christ of Latter-day Saints*, 6 vols. (Salt Lake City: Bookcraft, 1965–75), 1:257.

2. *Messenger and Advocate*, 2:199; emphasis added.

3. *Journal of Discourses*, 26 vols. (London: Latter-day Saints' Book Depot, 1854–86), 12:367; see also Acts 7:52.

4. *Journal of Discourses*, 19:24.

5. *Journal of Discourses*, 19:25.

6. Spencer W. Kimball, Conference Report, April 1981, p. 105.

7. Orson F. Whitney, *Life of Heber C. Kimball* (Salt Lake City: Bookcraft, 1978), pp. 129–31.

8. *Life of Heber C. Kimball*, pp. 131–32; emphasis added.

Chapter 2. If Christ Came Today

1. Hugh Nibley, "Early Accounts of Jesus' Childhood," *Instructor*, January 1965, p. 35.

2. "Early Accounts of Jesus' Childhood," p. 36.

3. "Early Accounts of Jesus' Childhood," p. 37.

4. Bruce R. McConkie, *Doctrinal New Testament Commentary*, 3 vols. (Salt Lake City: Bookcraft, 1965–73), 1:263.

5. Dallin H. Oaks and Marvin S. Hill, *Carthage Conspiracy—The Trial of the Accused Assassins of Joseph Smith* (Urbana, Illinois: University of Illinois Press, 1976), p. 6.

6. *Carthage Conspiracy*, pp. 213–14.

7. *Journal of Discourses*, 1:38.

Chapter 3. The Pharisees and the Signs of the Times

1. *Ensign*, November 1984, p. 67.

2. *Ensign*, November 1981, pp. 46, 48.

3. Milton Steinberg, *Basic Judaism* (New York: Harcourt, Brace and World, Inc., 1947), pp. 68–69.

4. For a more detailed treatment of Jesus and the Jews see Robert L. Millet, "Looking Beyond the Mark: Insights from the JST into First Century Judaism," *The Joseph Smith Translation: The Restoration of Plain and Precious Things* (Provo, Utah: BYU Religious Studies Center, 1985).

5. Dean C. Jessee, ed., *The Personal Writings of Joseph Smith* (Salt Lake City: Deseret Book Co., 1984), p. 298; spelling and punctuation corrected.

6. Joseph Fielding Smith, comp., *Teachings of the Prophet Joseph Smith* (Salt Lake City: Deseret Book Co., 1976), p. 313.

7. *Teachings of the Prophet Joseph Smith*, p. 275; emphasis added.

8. *Ensign*, May 1974, p. 72.

9. See a marvelous statement by Joseph Smith on this subject in *Teachings of the Prophet Joseph Smith*, p. 61.

10. *Teachings of the Prophet Joseph Smith*, pp. 320–21.

Chapter 4. The Bible Fraud

1. Gleason L. Archer, *Encyclopedia of Bible Difficulties* (Grand Rapids, Michigan: Zondervan, 1982), p. 19.

2. Harold Lindsell, *The Battle for the Bible* (Grand Rapids, Michigan: Zondervan, 1976), p. 18.

3. *Journal of Discourses*, 2:314.

4. Joseph Fielding McConkie, *The Spirit of Revelation* (Salt Lake City: Deseret Book Co., 1984), p. 78.

Chapter 5. The Weak and the Simple

1. *Juvenile Instructor*, 27 (1 August 1892): 472.

2. *Teachings of the Prophet Joseph Smith*, p. 268; emphasis added.

3. *Teachings of the Prophet Joseph Smith*, p. 368.

4. Bruce R. McConkie, *Mormon Doctrine*, 2nd ed. (Salt Lake City: Bookcraft, 1966), p. 309.

5. *Teachings of the Prophet Joseph Smith*, p. 278; emphasis added.

6. Bruce R. McConkie, "Are the General Authorities Human?" (Address given at the University of Utah Institute of Religion, 28 October 1966), typescript copy, p. 6.

7. Cited by Neal A. Maxwell in *Ensign*, November 1984, p. 10.

8. Spencer W. Kimball, *Ensign*, May 1978, p. 77; emphasis added.

9. Kimball, *Ensign*, May 1978, p. 77.

10. *Teachings of the Prophet Joseph Smith*, p. 258; emphasis added.

11. Richard Lloyd Anderson, "Parallel Prophets: Paul and Joseph Smith" (BYU Devotional Address, 9 August 1983), typescript, pp. 4–5.

12. Neal A. Maxwell, *Ensign*, November 1984, p. 11.

13. See James R. Christianson, "A Ray of Light in an Hour of Darkness," in Robert L. Millet and Kent P. Jackson, eds., *Studies in Scripture — Vol. 1: The Doctrine and Covenants* (Salt Lake City: Randall Book Co., 1984), pp. 463–75.

14. *Teachings of the Prophet Joseph Smith*, p. 349.

15. *Autobiography of Parley P. Pratt* (Salt Lake City: Deseret Book Co., 1972), p. 298.

16. *Teachings of the Prophet Joseph Smith*, p. 119; compare p. 160.

17. B. H. Roberts, *A Comprehensive History of The Church of Jesus Christ of Latter-day Saints*, 6 vols. (Salt Lake City: The Church of Jesus Christ of Latter-day Saints, 1930), 2:360–61.

18. Cited by Harold B. Lee in *Ensign*, January 1974, p. 126.

Chapter 6. Line Upon Line

1. Joseph Smith, *Teachings of the Prophet Joseph Smith*, p. 160.

2. *Teachings of the Prophet Joseph Smith*, p. 162; emphasis added.

3. *Journal of Discourses*, 19:12.

4. Letter from Joseph Smith to Silas Smith, 26 September 1833, in Dean C. Jessee, ed., *Personal Writings of Joseph Smith*, pp. 298, 300–301 (punctuation and spelling corrected); emphasis added.

5. From Orson F. Whitney, *Life of Heber C. Kimball* (Salt Lake City: Bookcraft, 1957), pp. 449–50.

6. See Bruce R. McConkie, *The Millennial Messiah* (Salt Lake City: Deseret Book Co., 1982), pp. 26–27.

7. See, for example, Harold B. Lee, "Be Loyal to the Royal Within You" (BYU Devotional Address, 11 September 1973), p. 90.

8. *A Plainer Translation: Joseph Smith's Translation of the Bible, A History and Commentary* (Provo: Brigham Young University Press, 1975), p. 86.

9. "The Jaredites," *Juvenile Instructor,* 27:282; see also *Improvement Era,* 8:705.

10. Cited by Harold B. Lee in Conference Report, April 1973, pp. 6–7.

11. *Teachings of the Prophet Joseph Smith,* p. 328.

12. *Teachings of the Prophet Joseph Smith,* p. 256; emphasis added.

13. *Journal of Discourses,* 22:35, 36.

Chapter 7. Fruits or Roots: How Shall Ye Know Them?

1. Hugh Nibley, *Lehi in the Desert and the World of the Jaredites* (Salt Lake City: Bookcraft, 1952), pp. 136–37.

2. *Deseret News,* April 10, 1978.

3. *Christianity Today,* October 11, 1974.

Chapter 8. Modern Korihors and the Art of Deception

1. *History of the Church,* 5:268.

Chapter 9. A Sense of the Sacred

1. *Teachings of the Prophet Joseph Smith,* p. 149; emphasis added.

2. *Teachings of the Prophet Joseph Smith,* p. 392; emphasis added.

3. *The Holy Temple* (Salt Lake City; Bookcraft, 1980), pp. 26, 30.

4. *Journal of Discourses,* 4:288.

5. Cited by Boyd K. Packer, in "The Candle of the Lord," *Ensign,* January 1983, p. 53; emphasis added.

6. *Clementine Recognitions,* III, 34; cited in Hugh Nibley, *Since Cumorah* (Salt Lake City: Deseret Book Co., 1967), p. 110; emphasis added.

Chapter 10. Wisdom in Response

1. Robert Bolt, *A Man for All Seasons* (New York: Vintage Books, Random House, 1962), p. 73.
2. Joseph F. Smith, *Gospel Doctrine* (Salt Lake City: Deseret Book Company, 1977), pp. 205–6.
3. *History of the Church*, 2:18.
4. Ezra Taft Benson, *Ensign*, May 1975, p. 65.

Chapter 11. A Household of Faith

1. *Gospel Doctrine*, p. 126.
2. *Gospel Doctrine*, p. 58.
3. Bruce R. McConkie (Address delivered at a seminar for Regional Representatives, April 1981).
4. *Gospel Doctrine*, p. 13.
5. C. S. Lewis, *Christian Reflections*, ed. by Walter Hooper (Grand Rapids, Michigan: Eerdmans, 1967), p. 46.
6. *Christian Reflections*, p. 47.
7. *Hymns*, #201, "There Is a Green Hill Far Away."
8. *Journal of Discourses*, 7:289.
9. Conference Report, October 1972, p. 176.
10. Conference Report, April 1970, p. 113.
11. *Ensign*, August 1983, p. 69.
12. "The Mantle Is Far, Far Greater than the Intellect" (Address to the Fifth Annual Church Educational System Religious Educators' Symposium, August 1981), p. 8.
13. Gordon B. Hinckley, *Ensign*, July 1973, p. 48.

Chapter 12. No Weapon That Is Formed

1. Bruce R. McConkie, *Ensign*, November 1984, p. 85.

Index